PRINCIPLES FOR PRINCIPALS

Principles FOR Principals

A Guide to Being a School **Administrator**

JOHN D. ROBERTS

NEW YORK

LONDON • NASHVILLE • MELBOURNE • VANCOUVER

PRINCIPLES FOR PRINCIPALS

A Guide to Being a School Administrator

Published in New York, New York, by Morgan James Publishing. Morgan James is a trademark of Morgan James, LLC. www.MorganJamesPublishing.com

ISBN 9781631954030 paperback
ISBN 9781631954047 eBook
Library of Congress Control Number: 2020951514

Cover Design by:
Rachel Lopez
www.r2cdesign.com

Interior Design by:
Christopher Kirk
www.GFSstudio.com

Morgan James is a proud partner of Habitat for Humanity Peninsula and Greater Williamsburg. Partners in building since 2006.

Get involved today! Visit
MorganJamesPublishing.com/giving-back

Table of Contents

PART 2: TWELVE GREAT GUIDELINES

ACKNOWLEDGMENTS

Now that I have just turned 72, I can look back and reflect on my career. I can honestly say that for the most part, it was fun. It had its ups and downs but mostly ups. Watching a graduation end on a happy note or winning the big game were always highlights.

I would like to thank my good friend, Mrs. Eleanor Jackson, who was my initial proofreader, critic, and mentor. She has been a great friend and has been encouraging me since 1970. She is an activist in PTA and was my former secretary at my high school for over ten years. Also, I would like to acknowledge several other folks: Ashley Thompson who helped me with my initial formatting, my wife Deborah, for proofreading, encouraging me, and offering countless advice, my son Christopher, for offering legal counsel, my daughter Jessica, thank you for your perspective as an elementary assistant principal and providing editing assistance, and my son Devin, for editing and being my chief cheerleader. **THANK YOU TO ALL OF YOU!** Finally, I would like again to acknowledge Mr. Richard Lukich, President of Constellation Schools. It is the management team for over fifteen schools and continues to be a leader in community schools in the state of Ohio. The community school has taught me a new compassion for education, student, and teachers—compassion in the belief that all kids can and will learn under the right set of conditions.

I remember when I retired from being principal for the first time. I had signed off the security code for the building and watched my replacement put in his code. I was no longer responsible. I walked through the cafeteria and said goodbye to the cooks and the custodians and got into my van and started laughing. Even though I realize now that all pressure from this job was internal, I could not help but feel a sense of overwhelming relief. I pulled into the driveway at my house and my wife greeted me with a Scotch and we both started laughing—the stress of being principal was gone.

This was a Friday and I was starting work on Monday for a retail company. I was able to set my hours. My wife gave me a list of about fifty things she wanted to be done around the house. The fifty items were done in three days. So, we switched roles and I became the stay at home dad who did laundry, washed and folded clothes, shopped, and made dinner daily. I also had the benefit of watching my kids play junior high and senior high athletics. I might have been the only dad at my daughter's seventh and eighth-grade basketball games.

Today, I am fully retired and living in Florida. No more snow days. Where will education be in the next twenty years? We have just experienced distance learning due to the COVID-19 pandemic and we are back to ground zero. When the paradigm shifts, we are all back to ground zero. Those school districts with vision will respond to this and create new solutions. Those without vision will flounder. To implement my vision for schools, it will take the cooperation of local school boards, the state's governors, and federal officials.

FOREWORD

I have known Mr. John Roberts since the early 1979 school year when he and Mr. Dave Laurenzi hired me to be the orchestra director at Valley Forge High School. Mr. Roberts was the assistant principal when I came on board and later became the principal. I would say that the hallmark of his building leadership was organization. He developed a procedure for everything down to the very last detail. When our beloved choir director passed away during a performance, Mr. Roberts coordinated faculty response to help counsel the students, organized the tribute and funeral to alleviate stress for the choir director's wife, and arranged all post-funeral receptions so that there was no preparation or cost to the family.

Mr. Roberts had the unique ability to be able to direct the orchestra, choir, and band as well as being able to call the offense on the football team. As an example, when my father passed away during the final rehearsals of our school's production of the musical Annie, he stepped in and conducted the pit orchestra through the dress rehearsals. His unique background in music, theater, and English made him a one-of-a-kind individual. His leadership style was one of doing what was best for the students in the building. His fair and consistent policy towards students and teachers alike was paramount in his building and he was generous and helpful to every department. The ideas and guidelines as presented in his book should prove invaluable to current principals and for those seeking to become principals.

It was a very sad day when he retired in 1999.

Dr. Randolph P. Laycock

Music Department Chairman, retired

Valley Forge Cluster

Parma City School District

INTRODUCTION

WHO'S RICHARD HIRTZ?

Not long after I became principal, one of my first tasks was to hire new assistant principals. While I would typically look for young staff members who were successful classroom teachers, guidance counselors, or other school leaders, I would also look to hire veterans who had worked a lifetime in the educational field.

One of my new assistants always rushed into situations without thinking. She was a former guidance counselor who was appointed to be an assistant principal. On this day, she looked and dressed like a professional educator. She proudly walked the halls, corralling kids, and getting them into their assigned rooms. Once on the second floor of the building, she could not help herself—she had to enter the freshman study hall that was just short of being chaotic.

The rookie first-year teacher was trying to take attendance like all good study hall supervisors. However, my new assistant thought she knew better and took over. Immediately, dead silence hit this study hall. She always called the students by their nicknames. For instance, if the kid's name were Thomas, she would call him Tom, David became Dave and Douglass became Doug. As she read the kid's names from what they had written on the attendance paper, she very emphatically called out — *"Who's Dick Hirtz?"* There was no reply and now she was on a roll. In her most authoritarian of voices, she restated the name, *"Who's Dick Hirtz?"* Once again, there was no response from the students in the study hall. Now she had my full attention. I was in the hall and heard her once again proclaim in a very loud voice.

> *"Who's Dick Hirtz?"*
> From the back of the study hall, one boy raised his hand, pointed to another student, and said, *"His does!"*

At this point, the entire study hall exploded into laughter and she quickly retreated from the study hall. As she passed me and my deputy principal, she gave us the finger and used the F- word. My assistant thought she knew better. The point here is that we all leap before we think, and we tend to take over before we realize what we have said or done. Develop an attitude so that you can laugh at yourself and have a sense of humor. You all know administrators that maintain a stern outlook and never laugh. On occasion, laugh at yourself or the situation in which you are involved. Do not leap into situations until you have a better understanding of the problem. Investigate everything. Get all the facts before you can remedy the situation. Remember to maintain your sense of humor and be able to laugh at yourself.

The purpose of this book is to give you my best thinking on a variety of topics. I was a public-school principal in Ohio for forty-one years. I served in a high school and an elementary school before I retired. I learned many lessons along the way that I wish someone had passed on to me. I believe we all learn from those who have gone before us, and I feel duty-bound to impart what wisdom I have about educating children in the 2020s and beyond to future administrators. In reading this book, I hope that you will become a great leader in your school and your community—a great teacher, a great administrator, and perhaps even a great person.

EIGHT GREAT IDEAS AND TWELVE GREAT GUIDELINES

MAIN POINT:

THESE EIGHT GREAT IDEAS AND TWELVE GREAT GUIDELINES WILL COVER A MULTITUDE OF IDEAS ON HOW TO HANDLE STAFF, PARENTS, AND STUDENTS.

After a lifetime career in the education field, I have finally been able to narrow everything down into what I call eight great ideas and twelve great guidelines. I was going to name them the Commandments of Education but that sounded almost sacrilegious. So, I came up with ideas and guidelines. Chapters 1-8 are the ideas and chapters 9-21 are the guidelines.

The first eight chapters focus on these eight Great Ideas. While I am sure that there are other worthy ideas, these are the ones that are important to me. These ideas are in the form of stories or experiences that I have gone through. Most of you will call these "traps to avoid"—traps that suck you in deeper and deeper and will only cause you pain and heartache as you go through them. The twelve guidelines will allow you to learn of my experiences in dealing with the school, students, parents and teachers. You will read about my successes and failures and hopefully be able to learn from my experiences.

Before I get going on the organization of this book, let us first pause for a moment and look at the word "leadership." What does leadership mean to you? My definition of leadership is **A PERSON WHO *SIGNIFICANTLY* AFFECTS THE THOUGHTS AND BEHAVIORS OF OTHER INDIVIDUALS**. There is a difference between leadership and management. You manage daily, but you lead your school through your goals and objectives. Leaders have high energy. They know how to handle problems. A good school leader can teach people to work together cooperatively and will always make decisions based on the best interest of the students. Leaders are risk-takers and are not always nice. They make tough decisions: and a leader is a good listener. You must give the impression of seriously listening to other individuals who are trying to relay information to you.

At this point, to gain a better understanding of leadership, I strongly suggest that you read Thomas Sergiovanni's book, *Leadership for the Schoolhouse: How Is It Different? Why Is It Important?* This is not an easy read, but it is well worth your time. The ideas and guidelines in his book will add to your overall understanding of school leadership.

I am all about avoiding pain and heartache. I often say that I get Novocain to get a haircut. But I have learned that emotional pain, often in the form of self-doubt, is much worse than physical pain. Once I had made a decision, I would dwell on it. Was it fair? Was it just? Was it the right decision? What I needed to do was to let it go. As principal, you will make hundreds of decisions daily. Most of these decisions will be good. But it is the one bad decision that you make because you did not think it through that will cause you emotional pain.

It was the first day of the school year at the high school where I was principal, and we had set-up an alternative schedule so we could have assemblies with all four grades separately. This resulted in an alternative schedule for the day. As we hit the lunch periods, I normally made a habit of hanging in the lunchroom by the cash registers and greeting students as they picked up their lunches. On this day, one of the union reps came up to me and said I had violated the master contract which guaranteed the teachers a fifty-two minute, uninterrupted, lunch period. This day they only had forty minutes. My reply to her was snippy, "You could stand to have less time to eat." (This person was rather large, and it is no surprise that she took great offense.) I apologized immediately. I had crossed the line. Since then, I have learned to keep my comments about a person's size to myself.

However, by the time I got back to my office, the superintendent had already put in a message for me to call her immediately. I did and explained that I had already apologized. Her response was she only wished she had been there to see and hear it. The result was a grievance that resulted in any changes to the daily bell schedule now had to be approved in the spring before the start of the next school year. In other words, you had to have a meeting with the Building Advisory Board to make any changes to the schedule. The lesson here is to keep your mouth shut and try to build consensus within your building.

PART 1: EIGHT GREAT IDEAS

GREAT IDEA #1
GET ORGANIZED

MAIN POINT:

THE KEY TO YOUR SUCCESS IS YOUR ABILITY TO BE ORGANIZED AND RUN YOUR BUILDING IN AN ORDERLY FASHION.

I believe that organization is the key to everything. The very first thing you should do as a new administrator is to develop an organizational chart of your building. Identify your assistant principals and their specific job responsibilities. Also, give them incentives to learn more about the overall management of the building. As these assistants progress during the school year, give them more responsibilities so that they become a more valuable member of your administrative team. This will help them to build their resume and prepare them for their next interview for another position in the school district. I feel that you are responsible for teaching your assistants and what it takes to oversee the entire building. You are preparing them to become principals and have their building to run. For example, let those who want to learn about writing a master schedule, study under the person who is doing that task. This will be another skill that your assistants may add to their resume as they try to climb the ladder in administration.

As principal, your primary duty is to steer the ship. Depend on your team to do everyday tasks. You are the one who delegates. You assign others to do the everyday tasks of the building. For example, assign developing the aide's schedules to one of your assistants. Assign another assistant the responsibility of who will be covering athletic events, plays, and concerts. As principal, you cannot be at every event or function. You must delegate.

In my building, I covered all home events. This meant I did not have to travel to away games. This allowed me to see more parents and have them see me in a social setting. For concerts and plays, I would greet the audience and introduce them to the play being presented or introduce by name the conductor of the music program being performed. Also, at the first concert of the year, I made sure that the program being distributed had a section on audience behavior and that everyone in attendance had reviewed that section. You may have to read this section aloud at the first concert. Students and parents need to know what is expected of them as an audience member. They are not at a rock concert. They are attending a formal school event and you need to educate the audience of acceptable audience behavior. As an alternative to reading the rules of etiquette, you could have the drama department develop a skit for the audience that exemplifies what is acceptable behavior at a school concert or play. Afterward, I would be in the back of the auditorium to say goodbye and shake hands. I would also have a police presence in the hallway by the ticket booth and once the money was put away in the safe, the policeman would patrol the parking lot. If we knew in advance that what was being presented was going to be a sellout, we would hire extra police security. Finally, we made sure we never left a student alone in the building after the show; the policeman and I would walk the hallways ensuring that everyone was gone and off the property before we left and locked up the building.

I tried to maximize my time while at these events. Most of my communications came in the form of emails. There were emails, phone calls, notes to be read or redirected, letters to be signed, and memos to be proofread. When I arrived at my school for an event, before I headed toward the event, I first stopped at my office and immediately reviewed the paperwork on my desk. I would go through each item one at a time and either forward various items or put them on my to-do list on my desk. Secondly, I would keep the items that needed to be signed and save it for the concert that night.

I would take the signature file with me to the concert and sign whatever needed to be signed while I listened to the performance. I would sign every letter individually. At the end of each athletic season, each athlete's certificate needed to be signed. I would sign each certificate. If a student started football practice on August first and completed a season in early November; he deserved an original signature on his certificate. I did not use my signature stamp. NO STAMP. This is all called time management. Everyone has the same twenty-four hours in a day. It is how you manage your time that will show where your priorities are in your school. You must decide what is most important. This is just one example of killing two birds with one stone.

The next thing is to get a firm handle on meeting with various groups in your building. Are the cooks more important than the custodial staff? Is the teacher with a PhD more important than the first-year teacher? Should the secretaries be looked down upon? The answer is no. Everyone is equally important, and you should treat them as such. One way to demonstrate equal treatment is to greet everyone in your employ by name. Learning the names of everyone in your school sounds crazy? I had a staff of 150 teachers and a total of 215 employees for which I was responsible. The student body numbered 1,500. How could I possibly learn everyone's name and position? To learn all these names, I relied on previous yearbooks to study the teachers' pictures and names. Then, I had to get out of my office. I would walk around the entire building at least three times a day. During these walks, I would meet and greet teachers and non-certified employees by name. This helped me to not only be visible to the student body but to simultaneously develop a rapport with the staff, as well. I also learned to memorize the student's names. By making the entire staff feel valued, the school functioned like a well-oiled machine.

When I met with my feeder junior high to learn about potential problems or students to whom I should pay special attention, they gave me their school's yearbook. I studied the previous year's yearbook to associate names with faces. A new freshman will be shocked when you greet them by name on freshmen orientation day, even though you have never met them before. It sends a clear message.

Another way I was organized was by having my secretary manage my appointment schedule. Since I am a visual learner, she would print it out for me. I always had a printed schedule for each day with all my appointments on it. I felt duty-bound to follow that chart of appointments and meetings and to be on time. It helped me stay focused. If I said a meeting was going to last an hour, it lasted an hour. We started on time and ended on time. This showed my assistants I respected their time and I was organized and able to structure my day in an orderly fashion.

Today, with the use of the computer, you can easily organize all your events for the year. How do we know which events go into the computer? You already have a list of events for the year because, to have an event in the building, you had to fill out a building permit. Have your secretary keep a calendar of all these events in a master yearly calendar so events do not conflict. This can all be done in the spring and the master schedule of events can be written during the summer. Before the start of the school year, meet with your administrative team, and determine who is going to cover which events. As I said previously, I was going to take all home events. Simply put, the assistants had to decide who was going to cover the away events. By having them select which events they were going to cover helped to empower them and make them responsible for that event. Now in the case of a big rivalry game, our entire team of administrators would be present. With 5,000-6,000 people in the stadium, you need to ensure that everyone is safe and that you are prepared for anything that might take place. Each of our administrators had a walkie-talkie in their hand and we were able immediately to send the police to a certain area of the stadium where there might be disruption. In most cases, the students were intimidated by having our entire team there that just simply seeing us stopped many disruptions.

Just one example: a student came to the football game intoxicated. I called his mother from the stadium and she came to get him. We advised her to take him to the hospital, but she insisted that her child had not been drinking. As we were discussing what to do, her kid threw up in her brand-new convertible in the passenger's seat twice.

She then decided to use the emergency transport (ambulance) for her son and they were off to the ER. She was even more distressed when I suspended her child for ten days from school. We always enforced the Board of Education's policy at school events, but we had the latitude to negotiate the suspension down if the parent was willing to work with us. In this case, the student went to have a private evaluation completed by a licensed psychologist and he received the help he needed. Again, we did what was in the best interest of the child—treatment versus suspension. You should have seen and smelled her brand-new convertible as she left for the ER. Very unpleasant.

Finally, you will have to meet with many groups of adults including: the alumni committee, the PTA, band parents, and adult boosters—each athletic team had a parent support group. Have a member of your administrative team attend these meetings and insist that the meetings be held in the building and not at a parent's home. Have the groups fill-out a building permit and you will have all the dates and times there for you to review. Also, remember that these groups have good intentions but need to be supervised. For example, you do not want the band boosters promoting a trip to Disney World when the Board has a policy of no out of the country or out of state field trips.

Speaking of out of country field trips, our district had a yearly trip to Europe to visit Spain, France, and Germany as a part of the foreign language department. On the Spanish trip, while I was principal, one of the students went drinking with a trio of Spanish boys and ultimately went skinny dipping in the local water display in the center of the city. The teacher in charge essentially did nothing and when she returned, she gave me an official office report and expected me to handle her problem. It clearly said in the trip rules that inappropriate behavior by any of the students involving alcohol would result in immediate suspension and the student would be put on a plane to return home at his or her parents' expense.

The problem here is that the teacher chaperone did not follow the BOE policy. Understand that the expenses for the teacher chaperone were built into the student's cost of the trip. The teacher received an all-expenses-paid trip to Spain, but she expected me to handle the discipline when she had the responsibility to follow the board policy. After this incident, I went to the Board of Education and recommended that there be no field trips out of the United States. I made this recommendation along with the other two high school principals in our district to show a united front to the BOE. Knowing what I know today, I would not take a child across the street to McDonald's much less Paris, Madrid, or Berlin. The risks are too great. No matter how good the kids and chaperones seem, there is always an element of chance that something will or can go wrong with foreign country field trips. When the BOE policies are ignored or not followed, it gives the impression that your school is unorganized.

GREAT IDEA #2
DON'T SAY "I DO" TO THE BUILDING

MAIN POINT:

HAVE A PERSONAL LIFE OUTSIDE OF YOUR BUILDING RESPONSIBILITIES.

Simply put, you can spend your entire life at the building. It can become all-consuming and you are married to your work. Being a principal causes you and your life to be put under the public microscope. You are not only the leader of the building, and the community, but a paragon of virtue, and moral leader of the school. Everything you say and do is looked at through this microscope.

There is a fine line that I would define as "having a balance in your life." **I DID NOT DO THIS**. Everything in my life revolved around my school. Even when I was on vacation, I was at work. People would bring their problems to me and once I listened to their problems, their problems became mine and I thought I had to solve them. They expected me to do it and quite frankly, I was good at it. My social calendar was filled with athletic contests, concerts, plays, proms, school dances, honors programs, band banquets, choir festivals, band shows, National Honor Society Inductions, open houses, and in short, any event had anything at all to do with high school.

As a school administrator, you are busy every day and night of the week and that includes the weekends. No one can keep up with this schedule. There must be a balance in your life. You need to take time for yourself and create this balance. Find a hobby. Find an outlet. Find something away from the building that interests you OR you will not be an administrator for long. You will burn out and you will **FAIL** miserably.

I distinctly recall a woman who was coming into the building to vote during one of our infamous school levy issues. She turned the corner, pointed her finger at me, and screamed, **"YOU!" "YOU!" "YOU!"**

"YOU ARE ALWAYS HERE. YOU ARE ALWAYS IN THE BUILDING AND YOU MAKE TOO MUCH MONEY BECAUSE OF ALL YOUR OVERTIME. THAT'S WHY I AM VOTING AGAINST THIS LEVY!"

The general public believes that we are hourly employees. She had no idea that I was in a salaried position and frankly did not care. She believed that I was an hourly employee and that my salary was based on hours. I took this as a compliment after I regained my composure and told the Board of Education this story in an executive session. It is very difficult to change perception.

We never know who is watching us or making what we do daily their business. They look for any excuse to vote against you and the kids because they perceive us to be only interested in making our financial situations better and that our motives for being on the job are strictly monetary. Our personal lives are unimportant to our staff, our students, and their parents. They want our help and attention when they want it. It must be on their terms, and they want it to work out in their perceived favor.

I often tell friends and colleagues that when we deal with our children, it is a matter of "we are only as good as our last purchase." Once our kids get what they want at that moment, they move on to the next objective. When they are little, it is easy to be a hero and give in to their every desire and whim. As they get older, the costs become larger and we end up extending ourselves to meet their demands.

It is always easy to say yes. It is very difficult to say no. Do not marry your job. Marry your spouse and be sure to strike a balance between work and home. Take a vacation. Take a night off. Take time for yourself. Rely on your family as your primary support system. If the school is organized, well managed, and supervised, you can trust that the ship will continue to sail. You trained your assistants and they should be able to handle any problems that arise. According to Harry Wong, a leading educator of educators and co-author of the popular book, *The First Days of Schools*,[1] we set up the rules and procedures. Then we practice the procedures until they are learned by the student body and staff. The school will not fail if you take a day or a week off. As they say in the theater, "the show must go on," and it will.

I have always enjoyed the movie, *It's a Wonderful Life*, and the character of George Bailey. George had the notion that he did not want to live and wished that Clarence, his angel, would make his life disappear. What George discovered was that each person's life touches many others. We do not know how what we do or say today will affect someone else tomorrow, next week, or thirty years from now.

Think about how many times you have said "it's a small world" about how each of us knows someone who knows someone else. Right after my good friend, our choir director, collapsed and died at an out of town choral festival, in front of our choir and the entire audience. I immediately went to the stage and tried to console our kids. First, when I got to the hospital, the choir director had already been pronounced dead. I consoled his wife and two children, made sure that they were okay to drive home, and then took off to get back to school.

---

1 Harry K. and Rosemary Wong, *The First Days of School: How to Be an Effective Teacher* (Mountainview, CA: Harry K. Wong Publications, Inc., 2009) Pages 175-179.

I also called my former boss who had just retired and asked him to meet the bus that was headed back to our school. I scheduled a faculty meeting for the next morning at 7:15 am to let the staff know what happened the previous night. I learned a stunning lesson that night. School life goes on whether you want it to or not. There was a substitute in this teacher's classroom the next day. No matter how valuable you think you are, the school will go on without you. We are all expendable. After the faculty meeting, I had to make arrangements for the school choir to be at the church on Monday morning for the funeral mass. After the graveside ceremony, we held a reception at the local community theater for a meet and greet with the family. Individuals from the community gathered up the necessary money for party trays and beverages. This went on till about 6:00 pm. When we go into full crisis mode, we also go on automatic pilot. We say and do the right things. Understand I had only been principal for about three weeks when this happened. What a way to start your principalship. After this untimely death, I had to interview and select his replacement. After the interviews, I was vacationing with friends on the island of St. John in the Caribbean and was on a remote part of the island walking down a very secluded beach. About thirty yards down the beach, a couple of scuba divers were emerging from the water. I turned to one of my friends and asked, "Wouldn't it be wild if we knew these people?" Lo and behold, one of the scuba divers was one of the people I had interviewed the previous week. Twenty-five hundred miles away from home and I accidentally bumped into someone I knew.

To quote the King in *The King and I*, "*So Big A World*."[2] As we get older, the world gets smaller and smaller. We are touched by so many people; it is truly amazing. Since I retired, I now live in Florida in a golf cart community. I have a big Ohio State sticker on my golf cart, and one day, a gentleman stopped his cart and asked me where I was from. You guessed it; he was from the same town where I had been principal. His son had graduated from my high school about twenty-five years ago. He even quoted something to me that I said in my graduation speech—you never know who is watching or listening. The bottom line is always to be careful.

One of my football coaches, who was a colleague and a friend, always said to me, "Take time to smell the roses." He died about twelve years ago from diabetes. I had lost contact with him as he had retired and moved out of state. However, he was very wise.

STOP AND SMELL THE ROSES. TAKE TIME FOR YOURSELF. TAKE TIME FOR YOUR FAMILIES. TAKE TIME FOR THE PEOPLE THAT YOU LOVE AND WHO LOVE YOU FOR JUST BEING YOU. YOU DO NOT GET A SECOND CHANCE AT LIFE.

---

2   *The King and I*, music by Richard Rodgers and lyrics by Oscar Hammerstein, II, dir. John Roberts, chor. Diann Smith, con. John Roberts, The Cassidy Theater, Parma Heights, OH, June 21, 2002.

GREAT IDEA #3
MAKE A DECISION

MAIN POINT:

WHEN YOU ARE MAKING A DECISION,
BE SURE TO LOOK AT ALL OF THE
RAMIFICATIONS OF YOUR DECISION.

Deciding something is difficult at best. You will be second-guessed by everyone whether you made the wrong decision. Ultimately, the one factor that I used was this: "Is this in the best interest of the children?" Some staff members may lose sight of the fact that the student's needs should be put first. Putting the needs of the students first is the first step in school improvement. Now, what do I mean by that?

Assuming that your best teachers are the ones who get the most out of their students, who should logically teach the Level One or slowest learners? The best teachers of course. My philosophy was that you should get a little of each learning level in their teaching schedule. For example, if you taught two advanced classes, you should also teach two Level One classes. My personal belief is that advanced students will learn despite whoever the teacher is and that it takes a lot more talent to teach students who are lower-level learners and do not wish to be taught.

With that in mind, building a master schedule becomes quite easy. Instruct your assistant principal and department chairs, to share the wealth when it comes to laying out a schedule. Again, I was always amazed at teachers who demanded that they have a certain period off. What does it matter if you teach eighth period or have it as a prep period? You are still due in the building and required to be there. Better yet is the teacher who insists they eat fifth period. Why? Because their friends eat then. Is this in the best interest of the student? Once you start to make exceptions for any staff member, you have lost the war because you cannot justify this.

Let us move on to how fast a decision should be made. You can rush through and make a poor decision, or you can try to look at the consequences of your decision before you implement it. I always tried to sleep on it and wait until the next day if I could. Because once the decision is made, it is extremely difficult to go back and change it. If you have a team of administrators, have a team meeting, and get everyone's input and opinion. At least you will have a united front as you move forward. The master schedule is only one example of an annual event that you need to plan. The process starts in February and ends in June. It is the events that arise suddenly and without warning that will be taking up your time. The water pipe breaks in room 101. The pool chlorination level is out of whack. The oven in the cafeteria stopped working. While you are not responsible for any of these crises, as principal, you will need to make appropriate and quick decisions to fix these problems. This skill on how to react to a problem will get easier over time as you gain experience.

With all of that in mind, when you decide to change an event in the building that has been traditionally been done a certain way, proceed with caution. Form a committee of teachers, parents, and students to study all the pros and cons of the change- as there is safety in numbers. If you decide to proceed with this change, do a post-follow-up on how the event changed and how the change was received.

In the early 1980s we decided to move our commencement exercise from downtown Cleveland to the local ice rink. We had looked for several years for a better site, and we finally realized that the local town's rink was available. We also gained the help of all the Parma Hts. Central staff. The ice was removed, and we rented 2,600 chairs that were put over a massive tarp. When added to the permanent seating in the rink, we had room for 4,500 people. Parking was free and families were given eight tickets each. The commencement went off without a hitch as the local police department handled all the parking and traffic and the local theater built a platform that could be used year after year for the commencement speakers. We also sent a letter to the parents of the seniors highlighting our rationale for this event location. Bringing the event to the community made it very intimate and personal.

The reaction of the parents was wonderful. In short, they loved it. Some of the parents walked to the commencement from their homes. We literally turned this into a theatrical performance. As the band was playing "America the Beautiful," the choir joined in with them halfway through the piece. The faculty processed in and the lights dimmed, and the American flag was lit gradually coming into full focus at the end of the piece. How did we get everything coordinated? Afterward, the superintendent looked at me and asked how did you manage to get everything so perfect? Using my authoritarian principal voice, I shouted, **"WE REHEARSED IT REPEATEDLY. OVER AND OVER TILL WE GOT IT RIGHT!"** Both students and parents were thrilled with the experience. The entire commencement exercise lasted an hour and a half and then it was done. The sense of accomplishment was tremendous. We all felt a great deal of pride as we had pulled off moving a major tradition by bringing commencement back to the community. After all the students and guests had left the rink, refreshments were served to those staff members who had participated in the commencement exercises. I took the remaining food and beverages back to the school and gave it to our nighttime cleaning crew. They really appreciated it.

With this story of moving the commencement, you understand it did not happen by accident. Remember, the committee I formed to approve this move, started the process. Thus, we were off and running. We notified the seniors and their parents what our rationale was and every chance I got, I would remind parents, they would not have to drive to downtown Cleveland and pay twenty-five bucks for parking. Then, they did not have to drive home from downtown Cleveland late at night. The civic auditorium was a large facility that could accommodate our large senior classes of eleven hundred students. Families sat in the balcony. My job assignment was to be in the hallway on my side of the civic center to prevent guests from throwing m-80s in the hallway.

As I obtained more experience, my duties were expanded to include just about every imaginable job associated with commencement. It all went back to the fact that we had planned carefully throughout the school year. After the event was over, we reconvened the committee to make a list of what went right and what we need to work on to improve it. We met numerous times with the theatre who was constructing our platform. We met with the sound and lighting people. And we met with the police. Simply put, we left nothing to chance. We developed a plan and executed it. The plan was rehearsed and reviewed. We spent the entire day of commencement at the rink starting at 8:00 am and we rehearsed throughout the day. Student speakers were given a time slot to rehearse. No stone was left unturned. Once we made the decision, the change was magnificent.

Remember, when I interviewed for the position, I had my own set of guidelines on how I would improve the building. This agenda covered everything from organizing faculty meetings, hiring of coaches, relations with the PTA, and improving commencement.

ONCE YOU MAKE A DECISION, THERE CAN BE NO EXCEPTIONS TO THIS RULE. YOU MUST ALWAYS BE FAIR AND CONSISTENT. WHAT IS IN THE BEST INTEREST OF THE CHILD IS THE MOTTO YOU SHOULD LIVE BY AND YOU SHOULD INSIST THAT YOUR ASSISTANT PRINCIPALS ALSO LIVE BY THIS MOTTO.

GREAT IDEA #4
BE GUARDED

MAIN POINT:

YOU NEED TO BE ABLE TO DIFFERENTIATE
WHAT CAN BE SAID AND WHAT NEEDS TO
BE TAKEN TO THE GRAVE.

D o not trust a great many people with secrets. **DO NOT TRUST ANYONE!** You will learn quickly who can keep their mouth shut and who cannot. Keep a very limited cadre of close confidants and only tell them what you want them to know. This may sound like I did not trust anyone. I confided in very few people and had very few friends. I was friendly with everyone but not close to anyone. This is a lonely job if you want to keep rumors and gossip to yourself. If not, you will gain a reputation as an untrustworthy individual.

I say be guarded because you must protect yourself. Once you have ascended to the top position in the building, everything that you do will be second-guessed. People will always look for an ulterior motive into why you did something or what personal gain you attained for making the decision that you made.

Even when you do something nice for someone else, your actions are still suspect. We had a fundraiser called Project Santa at Christmas time and we collected monies from each classroom and turned the money into gift cards. The gift cards were then sent to families who were on the Free and Reduced-Price School Meals. We used this list as an indicator of who might need financial help. Only my secretary and I knew the names of the recipients. I was the one who developed the idea of this fundraiser and our student council advisor did the leg work. Here I thought that we were doing a very good deed. Yet, we were criticized by many staff members because they felt that people lied on their free lunch applications. So, the receiving of gifts cards was unfair. But if we selected another group of individuals, someone else would complain. It was a no-win situation. The gift cards were for a store like Walmart because they sold clothing, food, and games. The card had a value of fifty dollars, and you could not buy alcohol or cigarettes with it. We continued this project throughout my principalship, and I received numerous letters and calls thanking the school for our generosity.

My best example of being guarded was when our school's business manager came to me and said that there was something wrong with our cafeteria accounts. We were short money for the number of lunches that we sold. She planned to put hidden cameras in the ceiling of the cafeteria and record everything that took place at the cash registers and where the deposits were being made. To that end, we needed to install cameras and recording devices and develop a six-week plan to carry it out. Only a limited number of people could know about this. On the day the camera equipment was to be put in place, we had the local police department do a practice run with their drug-sniffing dogs checking the building for drugs. This was done on a Sunday when the building was empty, and the presence of the dogs was a distraction from what we were really doing. While the dogs did their thing, everything was installed. I was only able to bring in one other person and that was an assistant principal whose office was closest to the cafeteria. When he arrived at school, he went to a locked cabinet in his office and labeled and switched out the tapes. I would pick up the tapes after school in my briefcase and put them in the trunk of my car. A guy from the security company picked them up at my house every Sunday evening at eight o'clock. Invariably, I had people over to my house for dinner. They wanted to know who this guy was and why he and I went into the garage together. They tried to get me to tell them and of course, they were the usual conspiracy theorists and the group guessed that someone from Washington was going to visit our school. This would not have been unusual because we had several visits from VIPs in the national scene. However, I made up some lame excuse and they bought it.

Six weeks passed and the tapes showed that money was being taken. The original team of individuals at the very first meeting met again in the superintendent's office and no one in the meeting could believe that the assistant principal and I were able to keep this a secret. They were in shock. They repeatedly asked how we do this. Our school district always had rumors going on and the fact that there were no leaks was amazing to the group.

It was quite simple—we never discussed it and we kept our mouths shut. However, there were ramifications because people now viewed us as rats for spying on our employees. We simply carried out the directive from the business manager. We merely followed orders. Was it a good directive? Who knows? The cafeteria cashier said she took the money to buy fresh vegetables for the staff and inflated the number of free lunch count to make the building look good. What seems like a good idea at the time may not have been. Today, I would have questioned this covert activity and maybe not gone along with it. Instead, I would have offered to discreetly interview all the cafeteria employees who handled money. As you get into these types of complex situations, be sure to look at everything and from all angles.

Being guarded makes it very lonely at the top. Decisions must be made and often made quickly. Some work and some backfire. Remember, you are not a god nor are you perfect. Being the building principal is a work in progress. When I started my term as principal, I had a ten-page agenda that covered everything I wanted to accomplish in the next four years. I tried to follow it but there were always interruptions by events that I never dreamed possible. I never shared this agenda with anyone as I liked the element of surprise when I implemented a new idea. For example, to start the school year, I had a lapel pin that I ordered from the Josten Company to give to the staff. This is the same company that you buy your caps and gowns and diplomas from. I had our vocational art class submit sample drawings of what the pin would look like. Then, my administrative team would select the drawing we liked best. It was then sent to Jostens to be manufactured. At the opening day meeting, I would invite the student whose drawing was ultimately selected to be in attendance at the faculty meeting and was introduced to the staff. I also gave each staff member a pullover coach's shirt with the school logo on it. We encouraged the staff to wear these items every Friday to promote school spirit.

YOUR TEACHERS WILL TELL YOU TONS OF CONFIDENTIAL STUFF IF YOU ALLOW THEM. REMEMBER, YOU ARE NOT THEIR PSYCHOLOGIST OR COUNSELOR. IF YOU

ALLOW THIS RELATIONSHIP, YOU WILL BECOME THEIR CONFIDANT AND YOU DO NOT HAVE TIME TO TAKE ON THIS ADDED STRESS OR RESPONSIBILITY. REFER THEM TO A FAMILY PSYCHOLOGIST OR THEIR MINISTER.

GREAT IDEA #5
CONFIDENTIAL INFORMATION

MAIN POINT:

WHAT IS DISCUSSED IN YOUR WEEKLY
ADMINISTRATIVE MEETING MUST STAY
INSIDE THAT OFFICE AND NOT REPEATED
TO ANYONE.

While this chapter and title seem very close to the previous chapter, I cannot stress enough that you will receive and hear a great deal of confidential information. Your assistants will need to be reminded that they cannot repeat faculty gossip.

You will probably have about a one-month grace period at the onset of your term as principal before staff started asking for individual meetings with you. I would suggest that you do the following steps during your free grace period:

★ Meet with each department.

★ Have them complete a questionnaire that you and your administrative team have developed. These questions should be as professional as possible. For example, what is your favorite subject to teach? Do you have any hobbies? You are trying to gain insight into this person and get to them better.

★ Once completed, you and the team review the questionnaire's answers and look for red flags.

★ In other words, try to plan and see which of your staff is going to be needy.

★ When assigning staff evaluations, assign staff members to each of the assistants as well as yourself.

★ Also, do the same thing with the support and cleaning staff; make everyone feel a part of the team.

Probably the most important thing to say to the staff is to keep their opinions to themselves and never use a student's or parent's name in a conversation whether they are in the community or the faculty room. I mention the faculty room because one day a parent came to see one of our teachers and the secretary paged the teacher but accidentally left the intercom on. The teacher, upon hearing the name of the parent, loudly announced what a pain a particular student and parent were. Can you imagine the reception the teacher received bounding out of the faculty room to meet this parent?

I also mentioned the community. Two of our teachers were in line at a bank to cash their paychecks and they were discussing their raise in pay due to the recent passage of the school levy. They were very loud and boisterous and managed to throw in a few words such as, "We really nailed the public this time." It took less than thirty minutes for this wonderful news to hit the superintendent's office because of course, they were wearing one of our school jackets. When I confronted these two about the incident, they said I had no legal right to say anything and they had the legal right under the Constitution to say anything they wanted, citing free speech. While they are correct, I tried to show them that some opinions are better left unsaid, at least unsaid loudly, and at the very least, unsaid publicly. I also tried to show them that we would need to pass another levy in the future and that their remarks were doing more harm than good. It is good to use common sense.

Back to confidentiality. I always thought what a great position it would be in to know all the dirt in the school district and be in on the front line. I was wrong—it is not a great position. You do not want parents of your teachers coming into your office asking for your assistance to put their man-child into a rehab unit for alcohol or drug usage. It is bad enough to have to engage a teacher who is doing a bad job in the classroom, let alone doing a bad job with their personal life.

One last story. It was the last day of school. The teachers were to be there until noon to complete their grades for the semester. At nine that morning the grade sheets were due into the office so report cards could be printed on time. We were under a time constraint to have our completed grade sheets into Central Office by half-past nine. Teachers checked each other's sheets to make sure that all the grades were filled out correctly and that there were no blanks on the grade sheets.

One problem—one teacher's grades were missing. We announced over the PA system that he should bring his grade sheets to the office. Again, no teacher. I convened our administrative team and divided up the building and did a quick search for this individual. Again, no teacher. About ten minutes later, three of the other teachers in that department came to see me to tell me that this teacher had been absent for the past three days and that the department was covering for him. I thanked them and called the teacher at home. There was no answer, so I left a message. I then called his sister and left a message for her to go and check on her brother. Then, I decided to call the police department for that teacher's hometown and informed them this person was missing for three days. By now, the sister had called me back and was headed to her brother's house. After about a half-hour, I tried the teacher's house again. This time the police department answered and informed me that the teacher had died and that they were treating his house as a crime scene. The police said not to tell anyone or discuss this case. Now my problem was twofold—what do I do about grades and what do I tell the staff? As it turned out, I already had the completed grade sheets from the teachers who covered up the absence. The police called me back later that morning and indicated there was no foul play and that I could tell the staff that he had passed but not to give out details. I brought this teacher's closest friends (a group of six) into my office and let them know what happened. I told them privately so that they would not have to hear the news in front of two hundred other people. That was the saddest end-of-the-year faculty meeting ever.

You never know what is going to hit you at school when you leave home. I have constantly referred to what I call The Jesus Syndrome, a phrase that I coined early in my career. This syndrome is the one where, as a teacher, we will try to save every child from every situation they will ever encounter. Throughout my career as a teacher and a principal, I had the opportunity to work with many children and their families. Many situations turned out very well, but others did not. While it would be easy to recall major successes, I would prefer to focus, for the sake of teaching from my experiences on what would become my greatest failure.

It was in the third decade of my career, that one of my students suddenly passed away. This was a student with whom I had worked for many years and he finally seemed to be on the right path. However, on New Year's Eve 1991, he passed away suddenly. I was extremely upset about this loss and I vowed that I would always go the extra step with other students.

Earlier that same week, my minister called me and told me about one of our church members. We were both ruling elders in the church. Her grandchildren had come from Texas to live with her and she was having custody issues with the school district because she did not have court documents declaring her the legal guardian. I said that I would get involved and see what could be done. Grandma had flown to Texas and rescued these two kids from an abusive stepfather and a mother who obviously could not (or would not) protect her children. Their biological father had disappeared after mom started dating another man and ultimately their dad completely disappeared. I had lost one kid, and this only made my passion to save other children stronger. I resolved to myself that I would help this woman and her grandchildren, who I had not even met yet. The story is even more convoluted when you get into the details of the boys' natural parents. Grandma had two daughters and her second husband had sons. Her daughter married her husband's son. In any event, their marriage produced these two boys. To get the school district to back off, Grandma had to get custody. I went through Children's Protective Services and Grandma was given temporary custody of the two boys.

The following Monday I met up with the boys and their grandmother. I was bound and determined to save these two young boys from their abusive situation. Without going into all the gory details, suffice it to say that I got into a situation way over my head and nearly drowned. The ultimate result was that the children were returned to their mother in Texas and they remained in this rather ugly situation.

On the surface, my motives were commendable. Help a child in danger. Help a fellow parishioner through a difficult period. I had rushed in to save the day just like my assistant principal did in the study hall. The only person other than the kids who got hurt was **ME**!! I had left myself vulnerable because I went into the situation with reckless abandon and got emotionally involved. I urge you to pick your battles very carefully. I urge you not to get emotionally involved in every case (easier said than done). I urge you to think the situation through and consider all the consequences.

In the end, you must look into the mirror and realize that you cannot save the world. **YOU ARE NOT JESUS OF NAZARETH. YOU CANNOT SAVE THE WHOLE WORLD.** You cannot stop suffering, hunger, cancer, or world wars. Like my assistant principal, I had rushed into this situation to be the white knight and I paid a terrible emotional price.

YOU NEED TO QUICKLY LEARN THAT YOU CAN NEVER REPEAT CONFIDENTIAL STUFF TO ANYONE. THIS WILL MAKE FOR A LONELY TIME IN YOUR LIFE, BUT IT IS TOTALLY

NECESSARY. YOU CANNOT TELL ANYONE ABOUT A STAFF MEMBER'S ILLNESS, A STUDENT'S DISCIPLINE AND THE LIST GOES ON AND ON. WHAT IS SAID IN THE OFFICE STAYS IN THE OFFICE. YOUR ASSISTANTS WILL NEED TO LEARN THIS ALSO, AND QUICKLY.

GREAT IDEA #6
MAKE YOUR BOSS PROUD OF YOU

MAIN POINT:

THIS IS THE PERSON WHO HIRED YOU AND EXPECTS YOU TO MAKE SOUND, COMPETENT DECISIONS. DO NOT DISAPPOINT HIM.

Whenever I interviewed for a position and I was asked what my most important goal was, the answer was simple—**to be a good team member**. The assistant principals need to be a part of a team of professionals that have been selected to lead the

37

school. The team's performance is directly related to the principal's leadership abilities. If the principal selects the right mix of assistants, the team will function beautifully. As a team member, you cannot put your immediate supervisor into a no-win situation. **NEVER.**

I had a superintendent ask me, "Why don't I get many calls from your parents?" I told her the answer was simple. I would just say to any parent who threatened me with calling the superintendent, "What do you think she can do for you that I can't?" With that said, the parent usually calmed down. I would then sit and listen to the parent's complaints and follow these guidelines:

- ★ I suggest strongly that you listen carefully and let the parent's complaints be heard.
- ★ Take notes.
- ★ Discuss it with your team.
- ★ Record the conversation. Use your phone to record the meeting. This little ploy will change the whole tenor of the meeting and usually calms down the parent because they now must carefully measure their words.

Usually, you are defending a staff member or another administrator's decision. Talk to them and get them to reconsider their decision. If they are wrong, you need to change the decision. Remember that not all situations are black and white. There are a lot of gray areas. For example, one of my veteran teachers dumped a cup of coffee over a kid's head in class because he did not like the kid. This act is a case of assault which could have resulted in a jail sentence for the teacher involved. The student did not get burned and there wasn't much coffee in the cup. Before the parents or their attorney ever had a chance to call me, I took the following steps:

1. I met with the teacher.
2. I had him apologize to the student in front of the class.
3. Then, I had him call the parents to let them know what happened and apologize.

My quick thinking not only saved the teacher from being charged with assault but headed off a potential lawsuit. Pouring coffee over a kid's head does not make me look like a good administrator but the preventative actions I took helped to resolve the misdeeds of this teacher.

If the assistant principals do a great job, it helps to create a positive building attitude where students and parents feel comfortable. I always put in my newsletters, "Please call me if you have a complaint OR a compliment." Believe me; no one will ever call with a compliment unless you goad them a little. You need to brag a little and boast about your school's accomplishments every chance you are afforded. open house, graduation, and awards banquets are a perfect place and time to list the good points of your school. When the assistants are successful, then I have done a good job training them. The parents believe that the school is well organized and running efficiently.

My high school was particularly good at getting kids to donate blood. I put it on the sign out front. I wrote about it in my newsletter. You must advocate and promote the good things your school does. You will learn to write good press releases and call the TV and radio stations when necessary. The newspapers and television stations will always mention a teenager's crimes and they usually mention what high school they attend. The misdeeds of one bad apple can color the opinion of the community and the whole student body gets labeled.

When I was principal at this high school, I would send out a letter to parents highlighting the various upcoming school events they might want to attend. Encourage people to mark their calendars and attend school events. Our kids work too hard to perform in front of an empty house. Involve elementary-age students in your school plays and musicals. They have a lot of family, friends, and grandparents who will attend and buy tickets. Our Christmas concert was a particularly popular event where alumni would come back to the building and join the Senior Choir with "The Lord Bless You and Keep You" after the concert. I had to bring additional seating for the back of the auditorium and ended up having to set up televisions in the cafeteria for the overflow. Great events like this only enhance the reputation of the building. In multiple high school districts, it becomes a competition between schools to showcase their students. Your superintendent will see who is working to make the district look good and who is not. By making your building look good, you are also contributing to the reputation of the district. As people leave the concert, be visible, shake hands, and wish them a happy holiday season or just say Merry Christmas. It is all a part of your job. Public relations at its finest hour.

Take the problem of the coffee-over-the-student's-head pourer. It was all handled in-house. We met the problem and solved a potentially volatile situation. The superintendent never got a call from these parents. It was handled quickly and discreetly without central office intervention. This does not mean that other parents will not bypass you and go directly to the superintendent. My superintendent would tell them to call me directly or the child's assistant principal. Everything you do and your staff does leaves an impression on your parents and the community. You make your superintendent look good by being fair and consistent.

BE YOUR OWN BEST ADVOCATE. ONE OF THE QUESTIONS I ALWAYS ASKED WHEN INTERVIEWING CANDIDATES FOR AN ASSISTANT PRINCIPAL POSITION WAS, "WHAT DO YOU THINK YOUR MOST IMPORTANT JOB WILL BE AS AN ASSISTANT PRINCIPAL?" I WOULD GET ALL SORTS OF RESPONSES BUT THE ONE I WANTED TO HEAR WAS THAT THEY WOULD MAKE ME PROUD BECAUSE I

HAD SELECTED THEM TO BE A PART OF MY TEAM. I EXPECTED TOTAL ALLEGIANCE FROM MY ASSISTANTS AND TRUSTED THEM TO MAKE SOLID DECISIONS WHEN DISCIPLINING A CHILD, MEETING WITH PARENTS, BEING IN CHARGE AT A SPORTING EVENT, AND MOST OF ALL, KEEPING THEIR COOL WHEN FACED WITH A CRISIS.

GREAT IDEA #7
PARENT RELATIONS

MAIN POINT:

RETURNING MESSAGES AND CREATING RELATIONSHIPS WITH PARENTS AND STUDENTS WILL ENHANCE YOUR REPUTATION.

I do not care how tired you are or how late it is, pick up the phone and return any calls that you received during the day. If you allow the parent to fester overnight, you will pay the price for it the next day. They will continue to call your office and harass your secretary. By not responding you have now managed to drag another person into this mess. Make the call and get it over with now.

If I were not coming back to the office, I would take my phone messages home with me and return the calls before 7:00 pm. If I received an answering machine, I would leave my home phone number and say call me up until 9:00 pm or I will call you back in the morning. This would usually diffuse a difficult situation. The parent knew I had called back and knew how they could reach me up to a certain point. It showed that I cared enough to reach out. I always took a chance leaving my home phone or cell phone number because their children might get a hold of the number and pass it on to other students. This never happened. I returned the call because the parent called me directly. I would listen to the parent's request and tell the parent that they needed to call their child's assistant principal. What do I do with the parent who continually calls after that? I would call in the assistant principal for that student and find out what was going on with this student. Why is this parent bypassing you and coming directly to me? I would remind them that they needed to handle this parent. If I took every call, I do not need assistants.

By returning these calls, you show the parent that you have received their message and are willing to discuss the situation. DO NOT decide on the phone. Get all the facts, involve the student's assistant principal and if necessary, meet with the parents in person. This shows several things:

1.   You are willing to get to the bottom of the problem.

2. You will mediate the conference and then turn the problem over to the assistant principal in charge of the student.

3. You are creating a rapport with the parent and student.

Allowing a parent to fester all night over the fact that you did not call them back will create a PR nightmare the next day. What you should always try to do is to make your day stress free and not have a parent attacking you with a verbal barrage in the main office. Always have coffee or some type of cold refreshments on hand to offer the parent. Sit with them at the conference table. Do not hide behind your desk and give the impression that you will decide with no input from the parent. Simply indicate that you are willing to hear their problem and make a fair decision.

Once you get all the facts out on the table, tell them that you will have their assistant principal get back to them by the end of the day with a decision. Thank them for coming in and wish them a pleasant day. Do not bypass your assistants in this process. Keep them informed and updated and have them attend the meeting if possible. Finally, keep a written record with the date, the time of day, the people present, and what was discussed. Keep this in a folder or on your computer so that you will be able to retrieve it if the family involves an attorney or goes to litigation. Speaking of litigation, we are in an era where everybody sues at the drop of a hat. Do not be intimidated by a parent that threatens this. However, I would do the following if they go this route:

1. Involve your Pupil Personnel department. Pupil Personnel handles all legal problems with parents and students.
2. Notify the assistant superintendent or superintendent.
3. Keep the Board's attorney updated.

It never hurts to communicate with Central Office and get them involved from the get-go. They will appreciate you for keeping them informed. Simply put, they should not read about it in the morning paper, without hearing from you first.

When I became an elementary principal in the charter school movement, I called every child's parent in the school during the first two weeks. If I could not reach them by phone, I emailed them. I chose the phone because I wanted them to hear my voice. Many of these parents were former students of mine who had elementary age children of their own. While calling every parent may sound daunting, it was making about one hundred and twenty-five calls over two weeks. It was a simple, "Hi, how are you, I am the new principal." This rather quick and informal welcome by me set the stage for a wonderful school year.

In this new job, I had replaced an individual who had been fired and the school was in somewhat of a chaotic phase. It just needed structure. I would visit each room every morning and did a conditioning exercise with the students. I would enter the classroom and put up my hand. This was their signal to stop talking and when it was quiet, I would say, "Good morning." Then the kids became so excited to stand up and say, "Good morning Dr. Roberts." I do not have a PhD. The children called me a doctor because when I would check their heads for lice, I wore a doctor's white coat and had a stethoscope around my neck. I would wear costumes periodically throughout the school year just to amuse the students and staff. After a while, I was able to learn all their names and greet them individually. All the rooms were connected, and I could easily go from room to room quickly. When I took a prospective new student's family on a tour, they got to see me in action. I quickly told my boss that if I could get a parent into the school and let them see it up close and personal, I would get them to enroll at the end of the tour. My teachers, staff, and students became used to having visitors roam through their classroom space.

As phone calls came into the school, I would answer them as soon as I could. The parent who had just called wants an answer immediately. Call them and deliver either good or bad news. **<u>BUT CALL THEM</u>**. Do not make them wait. It will only make things worse with the parent if you delay your response. A good way to catch parents off guard is to make random calls and leave messages about their child. Catch a student doing something good and call the parents commending the student. This to help lay the initial tracks in forming a relationship with parents. There is not a parent alive who does not like to hear positive news about their child.

Also, remember that many of your "parents" may be grandparents raising their grandchildren. They will need help and advice. Imagine being seventy-two years old and having to raise an eight or ten-year-old. **GIVE THEM ALL THE ADVICE YOU CAN!**

RESPONDING TO MESSAGES OF ANY SORT SHOULD BE A KEY PRIORITY. PEOPLE EXPECT AND DESERVE ANSWERS THEY SHOULD NOT BE KEPT WAITING. WITH ALL THE DEVICES AT OUR DISPOSAL TODAY, WE SHOULD BE ABLE TO ANSWER EVERYTHING DAILY. MANAGE YOUR TIME TO RESPOND IN THE EARLY AM, MID-AFTERNOON, AND AFTER DINNER IN THE EVENING. PARENTS OR COLLEAGUES MAY NOT LIKE THE ANSWER YOU GIVE THEM, BUT THEY AT LEAST THEY GET A RESPONSE.

GREAT IDEA #8
VOLUNTEER

MAIN POINT:

ALWAYS BE THE PERSON WHO VOLUNTEERS FOR THE TOUGH PROJECTS.

Have you ever been to a meeting and the superintendent asks someone to take on a project? Everyone's eyes immediately go to the floor and no one lifts their head for fear of being asked to run this event? This is when you should raise your hand and take on the project. Only an organized person can add one more thing to their plate and get it done—not only get it done but get it done well. Also, as the head of a committee, you can delegate and guide the project to your benefit.

This happened to me at one of our principal meetings with the superintendent when she needed someone to volunteer to head-up the Prize Committee for the Back the Schools annual fundraiser. The Back the Schools committee was the organization that paid for all the Levy campaign literature. No one in the room wanted to do this job. I immediately volunteered. I think the superintendent was shocked. I was able to procure artwork, restaurant gift certificates, and many other terrific prizes. But the best of all was that I was able to procure tickets to the Indians, Browns, and Cavaliers games complete with parking passes. The Back the Schools event sold out and was a complete financial success. All it cost me was time and a lot of phone calls. It also adds to your resume. You should keep a resume of all your achievements and update it as you complete various committee assignments and successes. You never know when learning how to write a master schedule will be just what another superintendent is looking for in their district.

At one point in my career as a principal, my high school needed new band uniforms. I knew that our Music Club was maxed out with fundraising, and our two band directors had 225 kids to handle. They simply did not have the time or the energy to fundraise for this type of project. I told them that I would head up the project with the guarantee that we would not sell candy, candles, or any product other than the band itself.

Our band was a source of pride in our community. We participated in Memorial Day events, 4th of July parades, and many other community events. My school was made up of two communities and I was well connected politically. The uniforms were about $300 each and this would take my best efforts to get this done quickly and efficiently. Anyone who purchased a uniform had their name listed in the athletic programs and had their name read over the PA at our fall football games. My first phone call was to the offices of both mayors of the cities where our students lived, and I convinced each of them to buy ten uniforms to kick off our fundraising effort. Next, I solicited from the fraternal organizations in our community such as Kiwanis, and Rotary. Finally, we organized a campaign to solicit from our band parents and all the parents in the school. Unfortunately, you must put your money where your mouth is. I bought a uniform. You lead by example. We had multiple administrators, teachers, parents, alumni, and school clubs donate to this effort.

After about three weeks of soliciting, we had raised the money. We did not sell any products. We sold the band and our music program. The uniforms arrived the day before the opening of football season and the band marched onto the field looking like a million bucks. Yes, I had called in a ton of favors that others owed me to do this project and it cost me a lot of payback. Now I was obligated to attend various political fundraisers at a $100 a pop for a ticket. My point is, whether you like it or not, you must work with your community leaders. You need to get along. You must have political connections.

This brings me to a list of things you must do in the community:

★ Be an active community participant.

★ Be seen in public.

★ Do not swear in public.

★ Do not drink in public, even in a restaurant.

★ Dress appropriately.

★ Always be respectful.

★ You are the moral leader of the school and must be held to a higher standard.

If you cannot or will not accept these terms, do not apply for the job.

Join a local church of your choice within the district, attend, and be an active member. Meet and greet parents at the social events after the service. Join a service organization like Kiwanis or Lions and become an active member. At each school event you attend, greet the people, and introduce the event. You are a one-man PR person and people always want to meet the principal.

One very unfortunate event will be the death of a student's parent or worse, you lose a student. You will need to go to the funeral home. You may even be asked to help select the casket and the clothes for the deceased. Also, you may be asked to speak at the service. You need to do what the parents ask you to do. You can and will do it. This is the hard part of the job and it is okay to show emotion. I would also suggest that you send a letter to the student and/or the family offering condolences. If a student passes, have one of the assistant principals gather their personal effects from their locker and offer to bring those to the family. It may be too stressful for the parents to come to the building.

We had a student go into the hospital and he missed graduation. So, we took the graduation to him. This student was a favorite of mine who did not let his physical disabilities stop him from going to all his senior activities. I believe he danced every dance at the prom, enjoyed the dinner that was served, and he continued into the night at the after-prom party. The result was a complete state of exhaustion and he ended up in the hospital. So, we brought commencement to him. In any event, I brought the superintendent and my assistant principals, into this tiny hospital room. We began the ceremony, complete with recorded music that was played the night before and, recreated the ceremony. I got to give my speech again and the superintendent declared him a graduate. We put his diploma in his hands and we were done. I squeezed his hand and he squeezed back. This was a sign to me that what we did was worth it. These are the kinds of stories that the public never sees or hears about.

I would later serve as a member of the board's negotiating team and would face the upper echelon of the union in their struggles to get money out of a rock. The bottom line is that the only things the teachers' union was interested in were how to increase salaries, improving working conditions, and lessening the teachers' responsibilities anyway they could.

The experience of being on the Negotiating Team caused me to quickly realize there are no winners in negotiations. No one is happy and bitter feelings will fester for years. My advice: do not volunteer to be on the board's team. It will take away from your time in the building and you will be doing your daily schoolwork in the evenings. However, if asked, accept, and listen.

Our team that was negotiating teachers' salaries with the teachers' union was headed by an experienced lawyer from a prestigious law firm in our area. She was methodical and would often predict how the other side would react. To my amazement, she was right most of the time. She was very creative in how she was able to manipulate the conversation to her advantage. One night during this period of negotiation, I woke up around four in the morning with massive pain in my back. I promptly drove myself to the hospital and learned from the doctors that I had a kidney stone. After about three hours, the stone passed, and I headed home. Once there, I quickly put on my suit and headed to the negotiations at a local hotel. By the time I arrived at the hotel later that morning, everyone from my team was at the bar having drinks. I said to myself that this was a good sign—we must have settled the contract. However, when I got closer to the bar, I was informed the teachers' union had given the board's team a ten-day strike notice.

The next day I received a call from the superintendent's secretary asking what I wanted for lunch and dinner and to report to the board office at noon. This was on a Thursday and negotiations continued throughout the afternoon and after a break for dinner, things started to heat up. Around two in the morning, we reached a tentative agreement. The sad part of all of this is that the two teams had resentments against each other and did not bother to even shake hands. I left the Board office and drove home. When I got there, it was about five thirty in the morning. I walked the dog and my wife came to the garage door and said, "You cannot go to school today in the same suit you wore yesterday." Even though it was now Friday and I was due at school in a couple of hours, I went into the house and told her I was just getting home from the negotiating session, that we had settled, and I was going to bed.

Negotiations will bring out the best and the worse in people. It is not easy. Nothing in education is ever easy especially when you are talking about dollars and cents. Negotiations come down to the personality of the teams. The teachers' union was made up of very experienced teachers who were trying to attain the best contract they could. They had spent almost a year in preparation for these negotiation sessions. The board's team only had a few sessions to prepare and we were totally under the guidance of our attorney. She made it quite clear that she was the spokesperson for the board, and as a team member; I was to say nothing while at the table. My input was to be given only in the executive sessions. This was probably the most stressful committee that I had ever served on and it took its toll on me both mentally and physically. The contract that we had negotiated would be in force for the rest of my career. I did not have to ever be on a negotiations committee again. I wondered if stress could cause a kidney stone.

Remember, as the building principal, you have been granted great responsibilities with powerful consequences for students, staff, and parents. You can hire and fire staff, suspend or recommend expulsion for a student which directly affects parents and the list goes on and on. It is how you implement these duties that make a successful principal. You can change an entire family's goals and lives. This is an awesome responsibility. Remember to do what is in the best interest of the child and stay focused on the children. If the negotiations led to a work stoppage by the teachers, the best interest of the children would not be served. Thus, our overall objective during the negotiation sessions was to avoid a strike at all costs. The teachers were entitled to a fair and equitable salary increase consistent with other local districts. We were able to achieve this goal and this contract was in the best interest of the students.

YOU CAN GET THE PROJECT DONE BECAUSE YOU HAVE A REPUTATION IN THE DISTRICT AS AN INDIVIDUAL WHO CAN DELIVER THE GOODS. ENCOURAGE YOUR ASSISTANTS TO DO THIS. THE PROJECT THEY TAKE ON COULD BE A STEPPINGSTONE TO THEIR PRINCIPALSHIP. THE BUSIEST PEOPLE ARE THE ONES THAT CAN ALWAYS TAKE ON MORE RESPONSIBILITIES.

PART 2:
TWELVE GREAT
GUIDELINES

GREAT GUIDELINE #1
SPECIAL EDUCATION

MAIN POINT:

YOUR MAIN JOB IS TO OVERSEE THE SPECIAL EDUCATION DEPARTMENT.

The role of special education in public schools has now spanned fifty years. I am listing the chronology of what I believe to be the key pieces of legislation that have been enacted. I strongly recommend that you research the following and read what the law says and how it is intended to be used. Become familiar with the terminology used in special education. If you are not familiar with these terms, become familiar with them before the school year starts.

<u>EHA</u> The Education for all Hand-
icapped Children enacted in 1975
<u>IEP</u> Individual Education Plan
enacted in 1975
<u>IDEA</u> Individuals with Disabilities
Act enacted in 1990 and reau-
thorized in 1997
<u>NO CHILD LEFT BEHIND</u> enacted
in 2002
<u>RTI</u> Research-based intervention
is known as Response to Intervention[3]

When I first started teaching, there were no special education students in regular classrooms. My school had accommodations for students with visual impairments and a teacher who knew Braille who would type up assignments for these students. There were no ramps for students with physical disabilities. Not only did schools not address the learning needs of special education students, they barely addressed the physical needs of students with physical disabilities. Changes started coming rapidly in 1975 and have been exploding ever since. Here is my advice on handling special education in your building.

---

3   Tim Villegas, "Think Inclusive," *Think Inclusive* (blog), June 29, 2017, https://www.thinkinclusive.us/brief-history-special-education/.

★ Hire the best teachers and people you can find for your special education department. These people should be compassionate yet demanding of these children.

★ If there are any accommodations on their IEP, it must be followed. **IT IS THE LAW**. If you do not follow the IEP to the letter, you are going to be sued.

★ Each student with an IEP should have an annual IEP meeting **and a three-year evaluation**. Some parents will come with an attorney to the meeting or bring a student advocate. These parents will do this to ensure that all their requests get put into the IEP as an accommodation.

★ Have one of your assistants or yourself at every IEP planning meeting and be ready to sign off on the IEP. These meetings may occur at any time during the school year and a reevaluation of the IEP can happen at any time if there is a change in the student's situation.

★ My special education department chairperson knew which teachers would be a good fit for a specific student. You need to make sure that students with special needs receive all the services that they are entitled to receive. Their teachers should be extremely flexible and have a pleasant disposition.

★ I would try to make the physical classroom where these students were stationed for homeroom as attractive and comfortable for them as possible.

★ Make it a point to speak with and learn the names of every student in the special education department. You will learn to love their enthusiasm and determination. They are just kids who want to be accepted. They have the same fears and hopes that every student in the building has. And you will find, for most students, their disabilities do not affect their self-worth or sense of humor.

★ One of my students had the accommodation of having his service dog with him every day. While his classroom teachers complained about the dog, their complaints fell on deaf ears. It was in the IEP.

As for preparing the home-based room, we had to move to a larger area. We found the perfect space—a large area with a kitchen and a place for a bathroom-we only had to relocate the vocational program that was currently using the space. Unfortunately, this was early in the era of accommodations and the school business manager said there was no money for improvements. Well, here we go. The students were getting stuck to the back of their wheelchairs because there was no air conditioning in this space. The business manager refused to buy window air conditioner units. He told my custodians that they were not allowed to put air conditioners in the windows even if they were donated. This is when I stepped in and sent the custodians to Sears and had them purchase three window air conditioners. The two custodians clocked out and installed them on their own time. Everyone was happy except for the business manager even though the cost of the air conditioners came out of my fundraising fund.

One final accommodation was there were no urinals or toilets in the closet. Again, the business manager refused to help with the financial expenses or the installation. He told me it would be too expensive to remodel this room. I had a great friend and parent who was a certified plumber. He was appalled at seeing this situation. He bought all the equipment and installed it over one weekend. There was no charge from him or his business. The closet was piped for a sink, urinal, and a toilet. The students no longer had to go through the kitchen area to the bathroom with their urine bag in tow.

My last piece of advice is to get to know these parents on a personal level. They will need your help and guidance with their child, and they will be facing a transition to adulthood.

AS PRINCIPAL, IT IS YOUR JOB TO SUPPORT THE PARENTS IN TRANSITIONING THEIR CHILD BEYOND THE HIGH SCHOOL SETTING.

GREAT GUIDELINE #2
TECHNOLOGY

MAIN POINT:

THIS IS AN AREA THAT CHANGES ALMOST DAILY WITH NEW INVENTIONS.

We have come a long way with the advent of technology in schools. I asked this very question on a quiz in one of my college classes—what will shape technology in the future and what is the next greatest idea? Just think of the accomplishments in medicine and research that the computer has put instantly at our fingertips. I think it is necessary to just take a moment to review where we have been and where we are going.

1968	Launch of Apollo 8[1]
1970	Canon pocket calculator, the Pocketronic
1972	Pong created
1976	Apple computer company
1976	First Apple computer
1979	Sony Walkman released
1980	Pac-Man released
1984	Macintosh was first sold by Apple Computer, Inc.
1985	Nintendo Entertainment System introduced
1990	World Wide Web introduced
1994	Amazon founded—opens online
1996	PalmPilot first introduced
1998	Google founded
2001	Apple iPod 5GB unveiled
2004	Facebook launched
2005	YouTube launched
2007	iPhone released
2014	Amazon Echo and Amazon Alexa

[1] David Gewirtz, "Technology That Changed Us: The 1970s, from Pong to Apollo," ZDNet, June 28, 2019, https://www.zdnet.com/.

Educational technology has helped to improve the teachers' delivery of instruction dramatically. With the invention of smart boards, whiteboards, and overhead streaming content to a mounted flat screen, the teacher no longer had to order a television cart and overhead projector. Teachers no longer had to run scantron sheets through a machine one at a time. Instead, school districts-built computer labs throughout their buildings. Students were given chrome books with the uploaded curriculum already installed. Students were now able to utilize virtual classroom learning using Zoom or Google classroom. This is quite a historical perspective. Look at how these inventions have changed our lives. How many of these inventions do we take for granted and use daily to communicate? Instant gratification is not fast enough today. We need information more quickly, and accurately. Two and three-year-old youngsters use computers daily to play games and learn. What does all of this mean for education in the future?

I believe that the future of schools will be a combination of distance learning and on-site learning. Children will be founded in the basics in grades K-3 with a massive emphasis on math, reading, and social skills. As you will see in the schools of the future, the delivery and pace of education will become much more individualized. Chrome books should be provided for students starting in kindergarten and updated as we move from level to level. There will be millions of websites to provide academic intervention in very specific areas and tailored to each student. This will take time and planning on the part of the teacher to match the intervention to the specific learning objective.

With that in mind, how does each school district operate technology? I believe that each district should maintain a team of technological experts who will be able to do the following efficiently and quickly.

★ Evaluate all computer needs for the district.

★ Order and upload all new computers to be ready on day 1 of school.

★ Have a technician on-site to fix and handle problems.

★ Conduct teacher in-services on curriculum updates related to new technology.

★ Keep the district-wide intranet running.

★ Attend the state Technology Convention annually.

★ Hire enough staff to repair all requests promptly.

★ Have sufficient storage and repair parts and pieces for all computers.

All of this will happen with the right person in charge of the department. The team of technology experts should have a technology director with the skill set to be a leader, teacher, coordinator, and above all approachable to all your staff. This person will make or break your system. They must believe in the mission of the school and be a contributing member of your staff.

With that said, the principal is the captain of the ship. If you are in a large district with a district-wide Technology Director, all your technology needs will be run through the district wide technology director. However, if you are in a small district, you will be selecting the tech director. Hire someone that you are positive can work with the staff. Give them perspective on what you expect. Do not be shy with this person. They can make or break you.

You do not need to know the mechanics of all the technology that you will have at your fingertips. Let the technology department do the research, recommendations, and teach your staff how to get maximum use out of the technology you have. Who knows what the next great invention or idea will be? I only wish I would have invented it.

Just imagine where we will go with technology in the next ten years just based alone on where we have been. Dreamers will have the opportunity to dream. If they can dream it, it can be built.

THINK ABOUT HOW QUICKLY TECHNOLOGY HAS CHANGED IN THE LAST THIRTY YEARS. A CELL PHONE IN THE EARLY 1990S CAME IN A SUITCASE. TODAY, WE CAN FACETIME, GO TO A MEETING ON ZOOM, AND HOLD VIRTUAL PARENT CONFERENCES. I STILL REMEMBER SOME OF MY TEACHERS WHO THOUGHT THE COMPUTER WAS A FAD AND WOULD NOT LAST. WHAT WILL BE THE NEXT GREAT TECHNOLOGICAL INNOVATION?

GREAT GUIDELINE #3
ATHLETICS

MAIN POINT:

IF YOUR SCHOOL HAS A LONG
TRADITION OF WINNING, THIS PART OF
YOUR JOB WILL BE VERY EASY. IF YOUR
SCHOOL HAS A TRADITION OF LOSING, IT IS
ANOTHER BALLGAME.

Your school will be in an athletic conference. It could be a large school or a small school conference and the athletic conference you belong to should have teams similar in size to your student population. Overseeing and running your athletic department will depend on how your district has your athletic department set up. First, there needs to be an athletic director in place. The athletic director should handle all day to day activities of the athletic department. If you are fortunate enough to work in a district where the Board of Education fully funds the athletic department, you are in great shape. It does not matter if you have anyone show up for the games and you will not be dependent on ticket sales to run the department. The athletic director will be responsible for the athletic budget, inventories of equipment, coach's evaluations, scheduling referees, payroll, and all activities that should arise. Keeping a close eye on the bottom line of the athletic budget is a priority.

I would meet weekly with the athletic director to review what games would be played that week, the administrator who would be in attendance for the away games, and to discuss any problems within the department. However, on the other hand, if you are in a district that makes you live by ticket sale revenue to fund the department, you have a problem. You are now dependent on relying on ticket sales to fund the department. Based on my experiences, this is what I recommend you do to fund the department if you must rely on ticket sales:

- Create an overall expense budget; have your athletic director do it.

- Ask the players to buy their home jerseys with their names on them.

- Create a budget for each team in coordination with the head coaches of each team, buying only what is necessary to run that sport.

- Create a 2-prong budget for equipment:
    1) what is necessary to run the sport
    2) wish list.

- Calculate the projected ticket sales income.

- If you calculated a projected positive net income, you could start to incorporate some of your wish list items in the budget.

- If you calculated a projected negative net income, putting you in the red, you have two choices:
    1) fundraise to cover the deficit
    2) sell more tickets.

Selling more tickets at the beginning of the school year is the best way to take care of a projected negative ticket sale income. At my school, we developed a coupon book ticket sales campaign. Before the start of each season, parents had the opportunity to purchase a coupon book of six tickets. Let us say that your single-game tickets were five dollars. Parents and friends could purchase a coupon book for twenty-five dollars. They would receive six individual coupon tickets which would save them five dollars over the gate price. You can get creative with this by offering a better price for buying more coupon ticket books. For example, if the family bought five coupon books, have them pay for four and give them the fifth one free. It would cost them $100 and they would have thirty tickets at a face value of $150. The coupon book tickets were good at any home sporting event. I would send out a letter to every parent as part of the back-to-school package an order form for athletic tickets. Also, we sold ads for the athletic program book and an individual page listing of parent supporters for fifteen dollars per name. Sell one hundred name listings and you have made $1,500.

A second way to take care of a projected negative ticket sales income is to hire five seniors who had just graduated; buy them a shirt that has the name of the school on it and the words "ticket salesperson." Have them go door to door in the neighborhoods in your part of the school district. This means you will have to draw up a map of all the streets that send students to your school and assign them to these five ticket sellers that you hired. I picked five seniors. You could pick twenty. The number of sellers is up to you. The more sellers you have, the quicker this is done. The week before they go door to door, write a letter that will be mailed to every house that you are going to solicit from and let them know that the kids will be coming to their house the next week with tickets to sell. I recommend indicating that you will only accept checks for these coupon books, but if they wish to come to the school, they could pay cash for them in the athletic office. By doing this drive, you can get a great deal of advanced income that will help you manage your budget. Pay the ticket sellers you hired, five dollars for every book they sell.

Once you have completed the budgeting process, monitor it very closely as a part of your weekly meeting with the athletic director. This will help you to keep an eye on how well you project attendance. If you are lucky enough to have a positive balance at the end of the spring season, you will have a carry-over to start the new school year. The key to budgeting is to always buy the best quality of whatever protective gear is necessary for each sport. I would recommend buying the best helmet and shoulder pads for football; if you get helmets and shoulder pads reconditioned annually, they will last longer.

The next area is coaches—hiring and firing. After I hired my varsity baseball coach to become the athletic director, he came to me one day asked, "Are all of our coaches a pain? Was I this bad as a coach?" Once you take control of the money, all coaches are your enemy. They will do anything in their power to get additional equipment or additional monies for something they would like to have. I would tell them that if they wanted it that badly, they should form a parent support group and raise the money themselves. This could be good, and this could be bad. What if the cross-country team raises a great deal of money and goes out and buys a beautiful warmup jacket and pants and they look like a million bucks? But the track coach refuses to fundraise, and his team is in rags? This will cause animosity between the student-athletes and their coaches and now you have a problem. Hopefully, your cross-country coach is also your long-distance track coach and these warm-up outfits can be shared. Remember, there is always a solution to any problem. You will learn quickly to think outside of the box.

When it is time to hire a head coach, the athletic director should do the interviewing with you. If it is a head coach for football or basketball, consider having on the committee a parent(s) of a graduating senior who will not be coached by the person who gets the job. The interview should be divided into several parts: there is the x's and o's part of the job, organizational abilities, recommendations from others, and the coach's personal philosophy about coaching. You should be sure to have their philosophy align closely with yours.

As you begin your principalship, you will likely start with a full slate of coaches. You will like most of the coaching staff, yet some may be more challenging to work with than others. The nice part about these coaching positions is that the contract is only for one year. You have the responsibility to manage your coaches and may have the responsibility to terminate them. I would urge you to meet annually with the entire coaching staff at the beginning of the school year. Also, if I were going to non-renew a coach, I would meet with them and tell them exactly why you were non-renewing them. Usually, your problems with coaches will occur over the discipline of the student-athlete. The coach will usually want to double-dip on his athlete. For example, the student-athlete is given his punishment by his assistant principal who suspends him for two weeks, but his coach decides to bench the kid for an additional two weeks. This is called double-dipping. You cannot do this. I had a coach who did exactly this. I met with him and told him he could not do this. He did it anyway. I immediately told the coach he would be non-renewed at the end of the season for dis-obeying a direct order from me. I should have removed him immediately. A very unfortunate situation.

Then, there is the coach who crosses the line with his student-athletes. I had a young lady who came to my office and told me her swim coach had molested her. I immediately called the coach and put him on a leave of absence, called the police, and had an interim swimming coach put in place. This process took a total of about ten minutes to complete. I had the young lady give me a writ-ten statement and to make a long story short, this par-ticular coach had done this in several swim programs in surrounding cities and was found guilty in a court of law and went to jail. What he did was a felony. He was a civil-ian. I use the word civilian because he was not a member of my teaching or support staff. As principal, you have much more control over a coach who is a staff member than you do over one who is a civilian. I define civilian as anyone who is not a certified employee of the school district. If you have no one on the staff that has the proper credentials to coach a sport, then you are forced to select from the civilian list of applicants. Whenever possible, always hire a staff member. BUT if you are forced to hire a non-employee, you must be prepared to interview this person and run an extensive background check complete with fingerprints. This will help to avoid heartache in the future if you have done your homework. By the way, my predecessor hired this person and he did not follow through with the background checks.

Athletics can be fun if you are winning but what if you are not? Then, you again must be creative with marketing. Offer a free sock hop after the big basketball game to anyone who was in attendance at the game. The kids will have fun and usually the adults who attended stay and enjoy it also. You will have to hire a DJ and security and you will need to stay and supervise the event but the long and short of it is that fans will have enjoyed the game and the after-game dance. Secondly, you can always come up with gimmicks at the game. You can have a half-court basketball shot and if they make it, they win a prize. The more lucrative the prize, the more the kids will want to be picked and try to make the basket.

The last item I would like to address regarding athletics is that at the beginning of the year your assistants will select what away games they will supervise. Please let them have the option to trade with one another as they see fit if they let you and the athletic director know of the change. The athletic director should be the person in charge of setting- up and running the home event. The administrator is there along with security to make sure that everything goes smoothly. I would strongly urge you to tell your security officers that they are not to leave the school until the last student is picked-up. If you are lucky, you will have one of your teams enjoy a great season and advance in the state playoffs. I was lucky. Our basketball team made it to the final four in boys' basketball. This presents a whole set of new problems. How do we get students to the game? Do we excuse students from school to go to the game? Do the students have to return to the school on the same bus? Who will supervise and oversee each bus?

You will have a million and one questions to answer but it will be a fun ride. Remember, winning is a lot more fun than losing. It projects to everyone that your whole school is a winner and enhances your reputation.

THE MOST LUCRATIVE SPORTS YOU WILL FIND ARE FOOTBALL AND BOYS' BASKETBALL. THESE TWO SPORTS BRING IN MOST OF YOUR MONEY FROM TICKET SALES AND IN TURN, THESE TWO SPORTS WILL FUND YOUR ENTIRE ATHLETIC PROGRAM. GIRLS' BASKETBALL HAS COME A LONG WAY SINCE THE MID-1970S AND WRESTLING AND HOCKEY HAVE DEEP TRADITIONS IN SOME SCHOOLS, AND THEY ALL HAVE THE POTENTIAL TO BE MONEY MAKERS.

GREAT GUIDELINE #4
PTA/PARENT SUPPORT GROUPS

MAIN POINT:

GUIDE THEM IN THE DIRECTION OF
WHAT YOU WANT TO BE DONE, WORK
FOR THE GOOD OF THE STUDENTS, STAFF,
AND BUILDING AND MAKE THEM THINK IT
WAS THEIR IDEA.

You need to be an active part of the PTA at your school as well as your district-level PTA. Volunteer to take part in these activities. This will not only help you be noticed district wide as a leader, but it will greatly enhance your reputation. When I started teaching at the junior high, I immediately joined our school's PTA and volunteered to be the staff member to be on the PTA Executive Board. At first, I listened very carefully at these meetings and discovered who the leaders of the PTA were. The PTA was dominated by women and you had to be very careful that you did not commit a faux pas. Remember when I said to volunteer—this is one position to volunteer for. It is very important to not only serve as a member of the PTA but to volunteer for the activities they are running. The ladies on this committee will see you in a whole new light. They will truly believe that you are a committed educator who can be trusted, and your word believed. My PTA had various fundraisers throughout the school year and their biggest fundraisers when I started were to have several dances during the school year. Naturally, I volunteered to be one of the adult chaperones. Usually, there was a dance-off, a dance competition between all the students, and the parents selected the winners. I, of course, was front and center with the microphone and I was the emcee who announced who the winners and losers were. At the time, I enjoyed these kinds of events. Today, I am long past the age of enjoying junior high school dances. I say leave this to the younger teachers.

As I moved up the administrative ladder, my reputation became one that if the PTA needed anything, I was their go-to guy. This resulted in my being surprised when I was awarded a State of Ohio Honorary Life Membership in PTA. This was an honor that the local PTA awarded to someone for outstanding work at the local level. In the 1990s, I was again honored by our PTA Council with an Honorary National Lifetime PTA award membership. I was honored and grateful to receive these two awards because it was unexpected, and it was awarded by my peers so I felt it meant more than another award or form of recognition might. I enjoyed being helpful.

My final piece of advice on dealing with the PTA—the State Convention. I had heard all about the wild times people had at the State Convention. It was held in Columbus and many had the attitude like the Las Vegas slogan—what happened at the Convention stayed in Columbus and would never be discussed back in the district. Simply put, this was a time for people to let go and do things they would not normally do. There was a lot of alcohol consumed at the State Convention. At my first State Convention, I went to the meetings and tried to learn. The rest of the principals saw this as a three-day party, non-stop. I was criticized by my fellow principals for attending the meetings, making them look bad, and I was carefully watching my consumption of alcohol so as not to do anything stupid. Need I say more?

The next item to discuss is support groups. Besides the PTA, you will have Music Club, Football Parent's Club, Adult Booster's Club, and various other adult clubs to support other sports. When I was principal, I would never let any of these groups meet alone and I would have an administrator at their meetings; by having an administrative person at their meeting, you are sending a clear message that you still are overseeing what the group is discussing and doing. God only knows what one group could or would do if left to their own devices. This does not mean that they would do anything wrong or immoral. It simply means that there are controls over what these groups can and cannot do. These groups are an extension of the school and you. The message to these groups is that you are the head of the school and the person who makes final decisions I had outstanding rapport with all of my support groups and they never did anything to embarrass me or the school. If the Music Club decides to sell fruitcake as a fundraiser, you better like fruitcake. This was a traditional fundraiser at my building and so it was approved annually. You will see this in my chapter on fundraising; go for the big buck.

Be an active part of the PTA at your school as well as your district-wide PTA. Volunteer to take part in these activities. This will not only help you be noticed district wide as a leader, but it will greatly enhance your reputation as a giver, not a taker. Is this important? I think that it is very important to be viewed favorably throughout the district. The only way to get to know parents from other buildings is to be active in the district-wide PTA. This is beneficial when you receive high school students you have already met at a junior high function-you already have a rapport with them. My Lifetime and State awards are prominently displayed in my retirement office. Remember how I talked previously about maintaining a balance in your life? I once left a PTA Executive Board Meeting because it was my daughter's birthday. At the beginning of the meeting, I politely asked the PTA president if I could give my report first and answer any questions from the members in attendance. You must prioritize your family first. Once completed, I bid them all farewell and got home in time for the birthday celebration. This is exactly what I mean about creating a balance in your life between work and home.

THE PTA AND PARENT SUPPORT GROUPS ARE A NECESSITY. THEY BRING PARENTS INTO THE SCHOOL THAT CARE DEEPLY ABOUT WHAT GOES ON IN THE BUILDING AND MAKING IT BETTER. YOU HAVE THE FINAL SAY AS TO WHAT THESE GROUPS CAN AND CANNOT DO. DO NOT ABDICATE THIS RESPONSIBILITY AND DO NOT LET THE INMATES RUN THE ASYLUM.

GREAT GUIDELINE #5
FUNDRAISING

MAIN POINT:

DECIDE AT THE BEGINNING OF THE YEAR WHAT YOU ARE GOING TO FUNDRAISE FOR AND THEN GO AND DO IT.

D o not sell a product like wrapping paper, candles, etc. but have an event that has a larger profit margin and where everyone can have a good time. For elementary schools, I recommend the All School Carnival. For middle schools, I would recommend A Night at the Races, and for high schools, a Reverse Raffle.

<u>All School Carnival</u>: Plan to have this event on a Saturday either in the fall or in the spring. There are companies you can hire to come in and run this event or you can do it yourself. This will take a great deal of planning and I would recommend that you do this kind of event in coordination with your school's PTA. So you do not have too many people handling money, sell tickets at the door that will be used to buy food, or to play a game. Develop a series of games that would be appropriate for each age level. Have a raffle for prizes that are donated to the carnival. Three or four hundred kids buying ten dollars' worth of tickets can fundraise several thousand dollars in four or five hours. Make going to the school carnival the coolest thing in the world. Have your parents and students bring their friends and neighbors. The more people, the more money you can bring into the school. This will be a long day for everyone, but the result will be a major fundraiser where people had some fun and you raised a lot of cash quickly. If you are bold and brave, have a dunk tank, and have teachers volunteer to do a half-hour stint. Of course, as principal, you should start the dunk tank by being the first person in the hot seat. Be sure whoever fills the dunk tank with water, that it is warm and soothing to your touch. Also, when you are in the hot seat, verbally bait the person throwing the ball at the controls of the dunk tank. People love this sort of amusement. I did this at our high school carnival, and I wore a football jersey from one of our rival schools. If I knew the kids, I would berate them verbally (in good humor) to try and dunk me.

Perhaps the school wants to buy choir risers, a new electric piano, sporting equipment, art supplies, etc. You should make enough in one afternoon to cover whatever it is you want to buy.

<u>A Night at the Races</u>: A Night at the Races is where a professional fundraising company comes into your facility and shows videos of actual horse races. We decided to have ten races and ten horses in each race; you can vary the number of races and the number of horses per race. The PTA will be selling naming rights for each of the ten horses in each race and then people will place wagers on the outcomes of the race. You should be prepared to make up a race booklet with the names of the horses and owners in each race. Then, the company will run all ten races and the evening will be over. I would recommend taking a break after the fifth race and have refreshments available for those in attendance. We generally served pizza, salad, soft drinks, and desserts. This is a fun event that can be held in the junior high cafeteria. The actual event is the culmination of all your pre-work. First, you sell a ticket to the event for $5. You will have a committee that will be selling tickets to the event, selling horses for each race, and finally, people who will take the wagers for each race. The parent who buys a horse gets naming rights and the caller of the race will use the actual names of your horses and the owner's names as they call the race. The school makes money in several ways:

★ Sell admission tickets to the event at ten bucks a pop.

★ Sell 100 horses at ten dollars apiece.

★ Split the betting proceeds. PTA gets half of what is bet, and the other half goes to the winning tickets.

★ Sell refreshments—pizza or a menu of your choice. You have very little clean-up and you have made a great deal of money quickly. With 200 people attending, you will have made the following before the event has even taken place:

Admission	200 x $10	$2,000
Horse sales	100 x $10	$1,000

That is $3,000 before the sale of food and splitting the betting. The company will run the ten races and the whole event is over in three or four hours. Your only expense is the company you hire to run the races. Your days of selling candy bars door-to-door are over!

Reverse Raffle: This is the best fundraiser you can ever have. A reverse raffle is a dinner/dance with a chance to win some big money. You should sell 200 tickets at a cost of $150 a ticket. Since there are only 200 tickets, each ticket has a number 1-200. The purchase of the ticket entitles the attendee to two dinners and a chance to win $2,500. You will need to pick a site that serves food, can seat 400 people, and has a liquor license. When I was working this event we went by the following schedule: The bar and selling of sideboards opened at five that evening, dinner started at six o'clock with a blessing and singing of the Star-Spangled Banner and the drawing of the numbers started at half-past seven.

Here is how the drawing works. There is a big barrel that has 200 pillboxes in it each containing a number between 1–200. The pillboxes numbers from the barrel are pulled out one at a time. Once your number is drawn, you are no longer in the running for the grand prize. Numbers continue to be drawn until you are down to five numbers. At this point, you stop drawing numbers. You will have five people left and they can decide if they want to split the main prize or go all the way. They all must agree to this process or we continue to draw until we have a winner. But they may decide to split the money. If this is the case, the next number drawn wins 100, then 200, then 300 and then 400, and finally the last number gets 1,500. It is nice when the final five agree and five people have won some big money (as opposed to one person winning all of it). Now that you understand the basic concept of the reverse raffle, let us get into some more details.

During the cocktail hour, I recommend selling sideboards. I always tell my bartenders to make their first drink a good one. This helps to loosen up the attendee's right hand and make them dig deep into their pockets and spend more than they might otherwise. One board might be five dollars a number and the payoff is $500. The house makes $500 and the last number drawn wins $500. You can have as many sideboards as you want but you must sell all 200 numbers. The sideboard number drawing corresponds to the mainboard. Let us say you sold a two-dollar, a three-dollar, a five-dollar, and a ten-dollar sideboard. That is a total of

$4,000. Half of that, $2,000, is set aside for prize money and the house makes $2,000.

Here is an example of what you can make:

INCOME		
Ticket sales 200 x $150		$30,000
3 sideboards: $2, $3, $5, and $10	$4,000 gross minus	$2,000
EXPENSES		
Main board pay-off		$2,500
400 dinners with bar $40 each		$16,000
Sideboard pay-off		$2,000
Misc. printing		$200
DJ expenses		$400
	Net Total Sales	$32,000
	Expenses	$21,100
	Net profit	**$10,900**

Now if you want to make this event extra special, you can raffle off gift baskets that are donated by different organizations in the school. Also, you should try to get forty gift cards worth fifty bucks apiece that will be given to every fifth number drawn. This makes the event a class act. Even if someone's number on the mainboard does not make the top five, they are still a winner because they won a gift card.

In review, to hold a successful reverse raffle you will need the following:

★ **Reverse Raffle Chairperson:** They should be a popular staff member that is universally loved and adored by your staff. I picked my head boys' basketball coach. He also emceed the event. This takes you out of the limelight, but you are still the brains of the operation.

★ **Main Board Ticket Committee:** Consists of head coaches and club advisors.

★ **Sideboard Ticket Committee:** People you trust. There should be no alcohol for the sideboard seller until his board is completely sold.

★ **Prize Chairperson:** This person should procure forty prizes with a value of at least fifty dollars each. These will become an extra prize for people eliminated from the mainboard. Every fifth number eliminated should receive a bonus door prize. The announcer should praise the donor of the door prize.

★ **Gift Basket Chairperson:** This should be a staff member who likes to decorate and arrange gift baskets.

★ **Raffle Ticket Sellers:** I would use my young teachers to sell the raffle tickets. This allowed them to participate in the raffle.

★ **School Treasurer:** They should be there with locked bank bags and keys. The deposit of money should be off to the bank as soon as the prizes are awarded. I had our school security accompany the treasurer to the night deposit.

★ **Venue:** You will need to book a venue at least six months to a year ahead of time. I usually renewed the place at the end of the evening for the following year.

This event requires a lot of detailed planning. My coaches were my key ticket sellers. I would tell them to buy their ticket and sell four more. Just doing that completed your table seating ten people. They will sell to friends, so they know all the people at the table. If the sideboards are selling quickly, put up additional sideboards. Remember the sideboard drawing corresponds to the mainboard. Once the first number is drawn, say it is number 100, all the sideboards remove the number 100 and that number is eliminated. When you get to the final five numbers of the sideboard, do the same thing that you are doing with the mainboard. Let the five final ticket holders decide how to split the money. Once the final five numbers are drawn, disburse the winnings. The school treasurer should distribute the mainboard winnings and each sideboard seller will disburse the winnings for the sideboard they sold. Your sideboard sellers must be people of integrity and honor. This event takes a lot of work, but it has big dividends if you pull it off correctly with the right people. You can charge more, or you can charge less for your main tickets. You can make a boatload of money in just a few hours. The key is to be organized. This sure beats selling candy bars and making only twenty-five cents per bar.

A Reverse Raffle is a wonderful event as it combines gambling with a dinner and open bar and in addition to a chance to for a couple of hours. If there is food left, take it to a food pantry. At the charter school where I was principal, we had a group of parents who acted as a food bank. They would distribute food to needy families in the school or their neighborhood. I took the leftover food to them the next day and it was distributed. Also, watch over the crowd to see if anyone is intoxicated and make sure they do not drive home. Tell the bartenders to lighten up on the alcohol starting at around half past ten and have the last call at a quarter to twelve. Also, be sure there is plenty of water and coffee available. Remember my rule: do not drink in public. This event is in public therefore you should not be drinking. (This rule does not apply to your wife.)

Now if you work in a district where you do not have to fundraise, you have found the perfect district. Do not ever leave that position or school district. However, even if you do not have to do it, fundraising has permeated the school atmosphere to the point of being unavoidable. I recommend having one of your assistant principals oversee any fundraising that takes place in your school. Have each club or group fill out a fund-raising permission form so that you do not have too many fundraisers going on at any one time. We always had a large group selling their wares at Open House. This was a great opportunity because our Open House was well attended. The Booster Club sold school jackets and various other adult organizations sold items associated with the school. Strudel was also a very hot item at this event.

Another quick way to raise money at a high school is to have a dance and charge the kids five or ten dollars a ticket.

You only need to hire a DJ, or a band and you have made a quick $3,000-$4,000 in just a few hours. Remember you need to have security and adults (teachers or volunteers—parents/guardians) to chaperone these types of events.

Lots of people charge for concerts. I never did this because I felt that a parent, who buys their kid an instrument and pays for private lessons, has spent enough. They should not have to pay to hear their child play in the school band. Ditto for the choir events unless it was a fundraiser for the choir. For example, we did charge for a renaissance fair put on by all the choirs. There was a dinner and musical entertainment that lasted about three hours. The kids were wonderful, and the cafeteria was full. Usually, the food was donated by the parents of the music club and so the result was a no expense 100% profit evening for the vocal students. We could go on and on about fundraising, but these should be enough ideas to inspire your creativity in creating fundraisers that are best suited to your school community.

THE FIRST THING I WOULD ADVISE YOU TO DO IS SEE IF YOUR DISTRICT HAS A POLICY ON GAMBLING AND/OR ALCOHOL.

GREAT GUIDELINE #6
BUILDING REPAIRS/ UPGRADES

MAIN POINT:

THE BOARD OF EDUCATION MAY GIVE YOU AN ANNUAL BUDGET FOR BUILDING REPAIR, BUT IT IS NEVER ENOUGH.

When I interviewed for the principalship, I had been in the building for fifteen years as an assistant principal and thought I knew every physical problem you could know about a building. For example, the cafeteria chairs were almost thirty years old, the ceiling in the cafeteria was falling apart, the courtyards were a mess, the gym needed upgrading and the list went on ad infinitum. It was a question of where to begin and how we could impact the appearance of the building. My predecessor had left me a great deal of money in our fund-raising accounts and I was determined to spend the money judiciously. I convinced the Board to fix the cafeteria ceiling when the mice started eating through the ceiling tiles and falling into the kids' mashed potatoes. It was hilarious to watch but it got the results that I wanted; once the parents started to complain, it became a priority to the Board. The cafeteria ceiling is fixed and paid for by the Board of Education.

I analyzed all our needs and set about making a priority list. First, I determined what repairs and upgrades were absolute necessities, such as safety concerns. I worked with our business manager and was able to get the cafeteria new chairs and tables paid for by the Board. I ordered navy blue chairs—the heavy kind which could not be easily thrown. I also installed two cameras, one at each end of the cafeteria. The cameras put an end to all fights in the cafeteria.

Also, I had all the lockers spray painted the school color navy blue because our school colors were navy blue and white. The lockers were their original color and looked dingy and chipped. Everything had a deadline of August first. All the lockers had long since had their locks removed and the kids were to bring their locks to school. My administrative team then brainstormed about a better way to issue lockers. In August, we started letting students pick out their lockers. The seniors started the process and would come in and hand us their lock and combination and they in turn gave us the number of the locker they had selected. In this way, if a student were in the band, they could pick a locker near the band room and it would be more convenient for them instead of leaving the locker selection up to chance. Once they had signed their card that indicated that the locker was the legal property of the school and we reserved the right to do a locker inspection at any time, we promised the students that their lock would be on their locker for the first day of school. In the evening, the custodians put those locks on the lockers selected that day. We did this every day until all four classes of students had the opportunity to select a locker. Selection of lockers began three weeks before the start of classes. Having the students select their lockers did several things. It was one less thing to do on the first day of school. One interesting thing that happened was when we started to bring in drug-sniffing dogs to search the school we discovered that all the drug dealers had selected lockers in the art wing of the building. These lockers were inspected, and those students had their drugs confiscated. Our administration team speculated that they chose the art wing for their lockers because there were multiple exits nearby and they could trade with one another for specific products. Students were suspended and arrested. We think this sent a clear message to those students who had a predilection for dealing drugs: **DO NOT SELL OR STORE DRUGS AT THIS SCHOOL!!!**

For one of our building upgrades, to further beauti-
fication efforts, I decided to display the pictures of each
of the presidents of the United States in one of our stair-
wells leading up to the second floor. I offered parents the
opportunity to purchase one of these framed portraits at the
cost of $50 a picture. The family who bought the picture
would have an engraved plate under the picture with their
names on it. This project sold out in less than a week and
my custodians had yet another installation project. When
your school is named for the winter encampment of Washington's Continental Army, how could you go wrong with
having patriotic pictures on the wall?

The next areas you must consider are emergency plans.
To quote Dr. Harry Wong, from *The First Days of School:
How to Be an Effective Teacher*, "You must have a procedure for everything and you must practice it."[4] Early on
in the school year, you will need to go over the following
with the student body: crisis plan, fire drills, tornado drills,
and active shooter lockdowns. Most school districts have
these as a part of the Board's procedures. You and your
administrative staff need to learn these procedures and you
need to practice them.

Assign each of your assistants to oversee one of these
plans and present all the policies to the faculty and staff
and review them. If necessary, read it to them. In a crisis,

---

4   Harry K. and Rosemary Wong, *The First Days of School: How
        to Be an Effective Teacher* (Mountainview, CA: Harry K. Wong
        Publications, Inc., 2009) Pages 175-179.

the faculty, staff, and assistant principals will have specific duties. These responsibilities will change during the school day because we do not know what period the drill will happen. They need to know where to go and how to behave. If you take these drills seriously, the assistant principals, faculty, staff, and student body will, too. Emphasize to the kids, that in the event of a true emergency, they will have to be quiet and listen to instructions. Again, you need to review and practice these drills and be prepared.

MEET WITH THE LOCAL POLICE AND FIRE DEPARTMENT. LET THEM HAVE INPUT AND SUGGESTIONS ON WHAT YOU SHOULD BE DOING. REVIEW THESE PROCEDURES IN YOUR ADMINISTRATIVE MEETINGS BEFORE YOU ACTUALLY DO THE DRILL. THEN EVALUATE HOW WELL THE DRILL WENT AFTER IT IS COMPLETED. KEEP A WRITTEN RECORD OF ALL DRILLS WITH DATES AND TIMES.

GREAT GUIDELINE #7
TEACHER EVALUATION

MAIN POINT:

THE TEACHER APPRAISAL WILL BE INVALIDATED IF YOU DO NOT MEET ALL OF THE TIMELINES.

Once again, as principal, you have the responsibility of retaining staff or firing a staff member. Firing a teacher is at best very, very difficult. Step one is building a paper trail and adhering to the contract. Let us start with some assumptions: you have 100 teachers. In this case, if there were four administrators in the building, each of us would get twenty-five teacher evaluations to do. I would assign the evaluations to each administrator based on their area of teaching expertise. I would encourage them to do their appraisals during the first semester so if there was a teacher who needed a second appraisal due to a deficiency there was still time to squeeze in the follow-up evaluation.

When you receive the names of the teachers you are to appraise, notify each of them and ask them to schedule a half-hour pre-observation conference with you. At this conference, you should get to know the teacher a little better, review their lesson plans and grade book, and discuss what they will be teaching during the observation. After this conference, you should set a mutually agreeable date and time for the observation.

On the day of the observation, get to the classroom on time, and stay for the entire period. Take notes on what you think went well or did not go well. If they need improvement, be specific and give them direction on how to improve. This is not a witch hunt: this is to help them improve. Finally, schedule a post-conference with the teacher to review the appraisal and have them sign it. Let them know signing the document does not mean they agree with you. It just means they are acknowledging you have reviewed the appraisal document with them.

Assuming it takes you an hour to do the observation, an hour to write up the appraisal, and an hour for the pre-conference and post-conference, this is a total of three hours.

For all the 100 teachers being observed, you and your team will put in about 300 total hours. This works out to be a little more than thirty-eight school days based on an eight-hour day. When you look at teacher observation through the number of hours you put into it, this becomes a very important part of your job.

A few more suggestions to follow:

★ Do not evaluate anyone who is a friend of yours. This is a no-win situation that only results in criticism from other teachers, or if it is a poor evaluation, criticism from your friend and possibly losing that friend.

★ Assign anyone who is at risk of being fired to yourself. You need to be the leader of the team. If you have all new assistant principals (this happened to me one year, all my veteran assistants either were promoted, left the district, or retired), do not give them the most difficult people to appraise.

★ Your building goal should be to complete all your assigned appraisals by the end of the first semester. The second semester will bring problems of its own. Creating the following year's Master Schedule will begin in earnest during February and March. Simulations will run in April and May so the finalized new Master Schedule can be completed by June first.

★ At your weekly staff meeting, review how many of the administrators have started and/or finished their teacher evaluations. Use Halloween as a reference point; if no appraisals have been completed by Halloween, everyone needs to start immediately and complete some by Thanksgiving.

Again, we are looking at a time management issue for your administrative team. They may need to stay late or take work home. The administrators are not contracted to have a specific time to arrive at school or leave for the day; I always wanted my team in the building at least a half-hour before school started and to stay till at least four in the afternoon.

★ My favorite time management strategy was to not go home between school dismissal and an event I had to cover that evening; I would stay in the building to get all my paperwork completed and messages returned, then, cover the event.

★ I would also use this time to work on a folder I kept for each month of the previous year's events of things that would be coming up that I needed to prepare for, such as record the Open House greeting at media services, edit it, and make sure it was good to go. On the evening of Open House, all the parents would be in their child's first-period class and they would be greeted by yours truly with a wonderful, pre-recorded speech.

★ During this time between school and an event, I would review other upcoming events, write notes of praise to staff members, communicate with the central office, and proofread any school publications, in short, anything that needed to be done.

★ I liked the idea of another set of eyes being on school publications, like the school paper or yearbook. You must try and stay a step ahead of the kids. Every year, you will hear or read about a yearbook that has been recalled due to obscenity or the editors of the book changing something after the teacher in charge of the publication signed off on it.

I am trying to give you a complete picture of what this job will be like. You will never get bored because you simply can never get it all done. Once you complete your work one day, and you believe you are finished; it will all begin again the next day. Remember to smell the roses. It is always a good idea to bring flowers home to your wife, not for a special occasion but just to remind her how much you love her.

One final note on teacher appraisal—there is more than one way of doing things. What about the teacher who regularly leaves the building without permission? I would videotape these occurrences on a time and date stamped recorder. Once I had at least a week's worth of footage, I would meet with the teacher and review my allegations. Also, I would have his or her union rep in the meeting. Of course, I would clear this kind of meeting with human resources and the superintendent. The superintendent is your boss and the person you report to daily; keep them informed and do not embarrass them.

Another example of a teacher leaving early is the teacher who has a second job. Are they working that job on their prep periods at the school? It is quite easy to prove if they use a school phone frequently at a certain time. Again, with the advent of cell phones, where everybody records everything and videotapes every fight in the building, it becomes more and more difficult to get away with anything. Ah, the best part of advanced technology.

A bit of advice for you and all your staff:

★ Do not be alone with a student at any time.

★ Keep your classroom door open when you are in the room by yourself.

★ I recommend that you stay off social media; I would not have a Facebook or Twitter account.

★ Only use your school email that the district provides to communicate with students and parents.

★ Dress like a professional.

★ Do not swear.

★ Do not ever let a student ride in your car unless they are your child.

As principal, you can only provide suggestions to your staff. If the above suggestions are followed, it will save your staff a ton of heartache.

READ YOUR MASTER CONTRACT AND EVERYTHING IT TALKS ABOUT RELATED

TO TEACHER EVALUATION. YOU NEED TO ADHERE TO THE GUIDELINES OUTLINED IN THIS DOCUMENT. READ THE DETAILS AND SPEND TIME WITH ALL OF YOUR ASSISTANTS REVIEWING THIS. FOLLOW ALL OF THE RULES IN THE CONTRACT TO THE LETTER.

GREAT GUIDELINE #8
CLUBS AND ADVISORS

MAIN POINT:

REMEMBER TO MAKE SURE THAT THE PERSON YOU SELECT FOR THESE NEGOTIATED SUPPLEMENTAL CONTRACTS IS QUALIFIED TO DO THIS POSITION.

Here we go again with having non-school employees apply for positions. You need to have control over these individuals. When you conduct your interviews for these positions, be very careful. You have much more control over the advisor if they are under contract with the board. If no faculty members are willing to be a club or activity advisor, you must be very careful in selecting a non-faculty member to be the advisor. Once you are named principal, you will have the opportunity to see who the advisor is for your active school clubs and what positions are open and need to be filled. I would always encourage staff members to start a new club in which they have expertise. Also, I would avoid starting a club that an outsider brings to your attention. New clubs and activities should be built around students' interest in starting a new club.

An example of needing a non-school employee would be if the drama director decides to put on the musical, *Oklahoma*. It is a heavy dance show and will require that you hire a choreographer. I would go to the local community theater and see who they used for their choreographer. Interview that person and have them undergo a state background check with fingerprinting. If they come back clean hire them. You have done your due diligence and you have protected the school and yourself. For example, of this would be hiring a gymnastics coach. You cannot just put the physical education teacher in this position. While it is true, they probably had one class in gymnastics as part of their college training, it does not mean they are competent to instruct students on the horse or floor exercise. If the student-athlete gets injured while performing in a meet, you have opened yourself to a lawsuit. It is better if you hire a gymnastics coach with experience from outside the school. You should check and see of your board needs to approve this.

Remember, the more clubs and activities you offer in your school, the happier the student body will be. We need to encourage students to participate in school clubs and activities. If all you did was go to school from eight in the morning till three in the afternoon and did not participate in anything else, you are going to say that school is boring. We want our students to be engaged as it has been proven that more engaged students perform better academically. At our freshman orientation every year, I would encourage the new ninth graders to be active participants in what we had to offer. For example, we had a terrific art department with teachers that the students loved and adored. We had over 800 students each year sign up for art classes. Now because of this huge number of student participants, we were able to hold an art show in the spring of each year. One of the art teachers came up with this idea. As principal, I made sure we had the appropriate number of display boards on which to hang all the pieces of art. We then had all the exhibits judged and awarded ribbons; each student received a certificate for participating. I had the Home Economics Department provide refreshments and had a string quartet play during the exhibition courtesy of our music department. On the night of the show, there were over 500 people in line to view the artwork. The student artists were there along with their parents. It was a very positive experience for everyone. I was shocked at the number of people who showed up for this event. The most important thing was

that many of the student participants had never participated in anything like this before. This was their first ven-
ture into student activities. It was a wonderful experience
for the artists and the people who attended. We also left
the exhibition up in our student center for the teachers
and student body to view the displays during study halls
and lunch periods.

My advice is to not be afraid to try new ideas. Let
your staff imagine what would make your school a better
place and go from there. Yes, it will create more work for
you, but in the big picture it will create a better learning
environment for students. The formulation of new clubs
and activities is an ongoing process. It should be based on
student interests.

As we head into the 2020s, it will be interesting to see
what clubs and athletics continue to strive and which ones
will die by the wayside. While technology continues to
grow at record speed, I believe that is where the students'
interest will go. Students will demand new clubs based on
utilizing computers. It could evolve into almost anything
and, as principal, you had better be prepared for whatever
comes your way.

Remember my motto: **WHAT IS IN THE BEST
INTEREST OF KIDS.**

A LARGE SENIOR HIGH SCHOOL WILL HAVE
A LOT OF CLUBS AND ACTIVITIES. SOME
OF THESE CLUBS AND ACTIVITIES WILL

RECEIVE A SUPPLEMENTAL CONTRACT. FOR EXAMPLE, THE DRAMA DIRECTOR RECEIVES A SUPPLEMENTAL CONTRACT FOR DOING THE PLAYS. THIS POSITION HAS BEEN NEGOTIATED BY THE BOARD WITH THE TEACHERS' UNION. YOU JUST CANNOT PUT ANYBODY IN A SPECIFIC POSITION ESPECIALLY IF THEY HAVE NO BACKGROUND FOR THE POSITION. THEY ARE NOT QUALIFIED.

GREAT GUIDELINE #9
SCHOOL PUBLICATIONS

MAIN POINT:

SCHOOL PUBLICATIONS ARE AN EXTENSION OF YOUR SCHOOL.

I am just going to give you thoughts for different publications that you might consider for your school: yearbook, school newspaper, literary magazine, and student handbook. You should utilize all the precautions that I will tell you about in this chapter. Remember, that you will be long gone from your position but the publications that are in print or book form will live on. You want all these publications to be squeaky clean. Let us begin with the advisor.

<u>Yearbook</u>: Hopefully, when you begin your position as principal, all these advisors will be in place and you will not have to worry. Other than the advisor of the publication, have a committee of two or three trusted staff members, proofread the publication very carefully. Look for anything that can be construed as immoral, offensive or bordering on pornographic. Student editors are very clever, and you need to look out for these things. Once the publication is proofread, who takes it to the print shop or mails it off to the publisher? Many times, the staff advisor will have the student editor do the mailing. This is a no-no because once it leaves the advisor's hands; the student editor could change all the copy and/or pictures. This type of switch out will cause you undue pain as, among other issues, it can delay the printing of the material and cost you quite a bit of money.

The price of hard copy printed material continues to soar, and the price of school yearbooks can become prohibitive. The real question is why do we have yearbooks? The answer is simple- we have always had yearbooks and we will have one every year. Now comes an important question, Is the yearbook about the seniors, or does it feature the whole school?

I would strongly recommend sitting down with the yearbook advisor and having a heart-to-heart. I believe the yearbook should be a compilation of all the school's events and should include a picture and message from the superintendent and the assistant superintendents. Also, the School Board should have a group photo and a separate photo of the board's president. If there is more than one high school in your district, the same pictures should appear in all the yearbooks. You do not want to slight anyone, and it is a politically correct format to follow.

One of the biggest things that bothers me with yearbooks is when a misspelling of a student's name appears in the book. Have multiple yearbook staff members review this either by reading the names back and forth to one another or by spelling them to each other. This is especially true for picture identification throughout the book. How can a student go through thirteen years of school and have their name misspelled in the yearbook? Try explaining that to a parent. The name spelling check should also apply to any programs that are printed for any event held throughout the year—concerts, plays, music performances, athletic publications, etc. Also, for the senior picture section of the yearbook, you might want to utilize a secretary who works in the twelfth-grade unit. They will be able to spot a misspelling of a name quickly. Also, you could have each senior review their name and have them initial that they have done so.

The next area of concern is the school photographer. Before you even start your first year on the job, your predecessor will already have a signed contract in place for underclass pictures and senior pictures. Written into the contract, will be a percentage of what will be returned to the school for all the money spent at the photographer's studio. Whatever money was returned to the school, I would put most of it in the yearbook fund to help alleviate the cost of the yearbook. The rest went into my principal's account to pay for awards. The senior picture packages can run upwards to over a thousand dollars per senior. If you have one hundred seniors spend this much on pictures, and you receive twenty percent of the $100,000, the photographer is still making around $80,000. If the photographer is good and has multiple senior high school picture contracts, they should be making a ton of money. Do not be afraid to hit up the senior picture photographer for something you might need at a future event. For instance, if the Back the School Committee is having a fundraiser, let the photographer provide an open bar that will be utilized at this event. This is a very small price to pay to have the honor to print photographs.

Your underclass photographer should have the same deal with students in grades nine through eleven. For the underclass photos, I lowered the percentage given back to the school and had the company offer a ten-dollar package to parents. My school was economically distressed and many of the parents did not have money to buy pictures; the ten-dollar package at least got them pictures of their child at what I would call a rock-bottom price.

Finally, you must consider if you want to sell digital rights to the yearbooks or other major events (graduation, senior concert). Remember, if you decide to start selling these types of items, find a staff member willing to run this so you're not contracting out to a non-school employee: hire someone you can trust but do not abdicate your authority.

School Newspaper: All the rules that you have for the yearbook, apply to the school newspaper. The paper of the future will probably be an online edition and student editors will constantly try to do controversial stories in it to see how far they can push the administration. Remember, as principal, you are the publisher of all school publications and have the final say as to what may be printed. Again, I would caution you to proofread everything in the student-run school newspaper multiple times before it is released to the public.

Literary Magazine: I would like to move onto the topic of the school literary magazine. You will always have one English teacher who thinks this is a worthwhile project. Having been an English major, myself, I thought that this was a very worthwhile project: it not only encourages your students to write creatively, but it allows them to get their writing published. Form a committee, to read the stories that were submitted, and from the submissions, select those stories to be published. I would recommend a blind read—simply put, there will be no student names on the submissions just a number. Therefore, the selection process will truly be based on writing merits. It will not become a political selection or a teacher's pet selection.

In the finished product, have a nice biographical section for each author.

In terms of marketing these products, you could sell them individually or you could create an order form where each of the publications could be ordered or a parent could order all three of the publications together. Of course, they would be given a slight discount for ordering all three. **REMEMBER, AS THE PUBLISHER YOU ARE NOT IN THE BUSINESS OF LOSING MONEY.** You could sell ad space in the publications and have a parent support page where their name would appear in the publication. If you charged ten dollars per name and you received two hundred requests, you just picked up an easy $2,000, all for the sake of a parent's ego and an intense desire to have their name visible to the rest of the school community.

Student publications can be creative or controversial. I would lean on the more conservative side with the layout and the copy that will appear in these publications. Again, long after you are gone, the publication will remain. Do you want to be known as the principal who had to have the publication reprinted after slanderous pictures or copy appeared in the book? You will be held responsible and you will have to eat the cost of reprinting. For those of you who do not know anything about publishing a yearbook, it is done in very specific steps. It is a continuous process that starts in August and goes through the end of April or if you are not planning to distribute the book until after the school year ends (August distribution), you can plan to have spring sports, the prom, the awards assembly and graduation photos in the book.

Again, if it is not broken, do not try to fix it. Try to follow the status quo with the publication and tread very carefully with new and radical ideas.

<u>Student Handbook</u>: The student handbook is a compilation of all the school rules and the school calendar that includes days off, teacher workdays, parent-teacher conferences, end of marking periods, grades sent out, and scheduled events for the year. You can make this as dull or as attractive as you want. I would assign one of my assistant principals the task of organizing the student handbook. They should form a committee to review the old handbook and see how it can be jazzed-up or if it is fine to stay the same. You could utilize student pictures throughout the publication but get a parental sign-off that they approve of their youngster's picture being used. Remember, an ounce of prevention is worth a pound of the cure. Look at other schools' student handbooks for ideas. Create layouts that make the students want to read this publication. Have the student handbooks distributed on the first day of school and have the student sign off that they received the handbook. This is their due process under the law that they have been given a student handbook. This will be very useful against an attorney who looks for every loophole in your system. At each grade level assembly on the first day of school, I would review with all the students any major changes to the discipline code since the previous year.

Speaking of due process, emphasize to your assistants that all students are entitled to due process. Verbalize to the student what offense they have committed and give them a copy of the office report with (or the assistant's) signature on it. **<u>DO NOT OVERLOOK OR SKIP THIS STEP—NEVER.</u>**

Your secretary should enter each office report into the computer and keep track of what happens from day one of the school year right up to graduation. Be sure that this folder automatically backs up somewhere. What once was a paper nightmare has become a computer nightmare. However, it is more reliable and certainly tidier.

I AM GOING TO GIVE YOU THOUGHTS FOR FOUR DIFFERENT PUBLICATIONS THAT YOU MIGHT CONSIDER FOR YOUR SCHOOL: YEARBOOK, SCHOOL NEWSPAPER, LITERARY MAGAZINE, AND STUDENT HANDBOOK. YOU SHOULD UTILIZE ALL THE PRECAUTIONS THAT I HAVE OUTLINED FOR YOU IN THIS CHAPTER.

GREAT GUIDELINE #10
PERFORMING GROUPS

MAIN POINT:

THIS CAN BE A VERY PRODUCTIVE PART OF
YOUR LIFE OR IT CAN BE A DISASTER.

At the beginning of the year, I would have a sit-down meeting with the following: band director, orchestra director, choir director, and play director. At this meeting, I would discuss the following: performance dates, types of performances, and what will be performed. I would also discuss student behavior.

Marching Band: Marching band begins in early August. I caution you to be careful of hazing. Just like with sports teams, freshman or upperclassmen, sometimes called probies, like in the Navy new to the band can be the target of hazing. **Hazing is against the law.** An example of hazing is where the senior members of the band wake up the new freshmen. The senior go to their house, wake them up, and dresses them in some type of costume. Then, they drive the initiate to the school and they have a breakfast for everyone. Seems harmless enough. But what happens if something goes wrong? What if there is a car accident or a student gets sick from the food that is served? The parents of an injured student will come looking for the principal. Did you know about this activity and did you approve of it? There are legal ramifications here and you must protect yourself.

In today's litigious climate, I would not allow it. Punish upperclassmen that do this and repeatedly make this known to the band. Even if the current members had to endure this hazing, it cannot be allowed to happen, and you need to document what steps you took to stop this kind of activity. Once you learn of hazing happening, and you do nothing, you are giving your tacit approval. You are setting yourself up for a lawsuit. If I were the band director, I would have the principal and/or the whole administrative teams meet with the band and review this policy to make sure it is clear to everyone. This is a great opportunity to meet firsthand with the band. The marching band is an extension of the school. If the marching band is a disciplined unit, it projects the impression that your school is a disciplined unit.

Usually, the marching band season ends when football ends, and the culmination is a band banquet with a program and where certificates and awards are handed out. This is a potluck dinner that the band members and band parents all attend, and you should, as well. The parents usually bring their best dishes. Do not forget the dessert table at the end of this event. Make sure that they have plenty of coffee, too. The band director will oversee this activity and may allow you to say a few words. Be sure to thank everyone, especially the Band Parents' Club Officers. When given the chance to speak, take the opportunity. It shows that you are the leader of the building and that you care about the music program. Always make sure that the program presented is G-rated and that there are no surprises at this event.

<u>Concert Band, Choirs, and Orchestra</u>: There will be many scheduled events during the school year. The more concerts that are scheduled, the more you must attend. Remember way back in August, when you said that you would take *all* home events? You will be the administrator in charge of these events. What exactly does that mean? It means that you will oversee crowd control, audience behavior, and emcee, or at least introduce the event. Right before the concert begins, take center stage and introduce yourself and the event. Then, introduce the conductor of the concert and let it begin. At this point, the conductor will introduce the various pieces of music that will be presented. Furthermore, I would recommend that there be a printed program. In this program, there should be a listing of the songs and their composers, arrangers, and/or lyricists that are being presented, members of the group by voice or instrument, a listing of the school administration, and a listing of the superintendent and the school board. Should any of these members be present at the concert, recognize them during your introductory speech and have them stand and be recognized. I would strongly recommend a section in the program on audience behavior. Put it in writing what you expect of the audience and what is appropriate and what is inappropriate. This could include audience etiquette everyone may not be aware of, such as applause after songs and not applauding between movements of a long song such as a cantata. You would also want to go over food and drinks, cell phone use, cameras, and flash photography, and getting out of seats. Not everyone knows, for example, to wait until intermission to stand and use the restroom, but if they can't wait until intermission, they should still wait for a break in the music and excuse themselves during the applause; on the flip side, an audience member may not be allowed into the auditorium by an usher until there is a break in the music. Behavior at the first concert of the year at your school should be much different than the audience behavior at a Pink Floyd concert.

Depending on the type of concert, you may need overflow seating. I would always have an extra bunch of chairs to put up in the back of the auditorium. Be cautious of the fire code and allowing too many people in and whether overflow seating would cause any fire code violations. I would hire police for the parking lots to help direct traffic and monitor behavior; once the concert started, I would bring them into the auditorium in case of disruption. I never expected the audience to misbehave but the mere presence of the police may be enough to stop something before it happens. After the concert, I would move the officers back to the parking lot to ensure smooth exciting traffic. At the end of our Christmas concert, we always invited the alumni up on stage to sing "The Lord Bless and Keep You." Yes, we sang a religious song in a public school. This was a tradition. All schools have traditions and you need to either allow or disallow them. I vote to keep the tradition.

Usually, after a major concert or performance, there was a party at one of the parent's homes. If this is a tradition at your school, I recommend stopping by the home before the party and seeing if they needed anything. I would usually bring five or six cases of pop (soda) to the house (paid for out of my fundraising account) and reinforce to the group attending that school rules would apply—no smoking, alcohol, or drugs.

GREAT GUIDELINE #11
SCHOOL-WIDE DISCIPLINE

MAIN POINT:

TELL YOUR ASSISTANTS, WHO WILL BE DOING MOST OF THE DISCIPLINE, TO DO THE FOLLOWING: BE FIRM, BE FAIR AND BE CONSISTENT.

By creating a school student handbook, you will have a visual document that outlines all the rules of the school. Your assistants will need to memorize this rule book as they administer punishment. They must be fair, and consistent with each student. There will be students they like and students who will be a bit more challenging. Do not let them over punish the students who are constant repeat offenders but work with them to make them behave.

Lots of schools use detentions for punishment. This does not work. The kids will cut the detentions and end up back in your office to get more detentions. Instead of detentions, I would use a demerit system. Once you hit a certain number of demerits, you would receive a one-day suspension either at home or in school. You can also use a Saturday suspension. Minor infractions should be dealt with using minor punishments.

In-School Suspensions: You could establish an in-school suspension room where the student reports to with their class assignments and they sit in there all day and do their classwork. If they are unable to behave in a reasonable manner, the in-school suspension will no longer be available. The in-school option allows the student to do his regular classroom assignments and receive credit for them. Parents preferred this option as their child would not be left home alone to serve an out of school suspension Remember that you will need to cover the in-school suspension room with supervisors. I would select supervisors who will help the kids with their work and not treat them like prisoners.

Saturday Suspensions: This was an option that I developed at my school. The parents of a suspended student could choose to have a Saturday suspension instead of in or out of school suspension. Parents would have to provide transportation and it was understood that their child would be picking up trash and general cleanup around the building. It is a privilege to have a Saturday suspension. You must have the parent agree to this punishment and sign a waiver. No signature, no Saturday suspension. In this case, the child is suspended at home under the supervision of the parent. I would afford parents the opportunity of allowing their students to serve the suspension on Saturday. This would be four hours spent with me. Each student would be handed a garbage bag and we would go out in front of the building and get two or three feet apart in a single line and pick up every bit of trash on the school property. Once we had cleaned up the front of the building, we would move to the back. Once the property was clear of debris, we would define the tree beds lining the front of the building and put down new mulch. This whole process took planning on my part, but the parents were appreciative that we had an alternative to at-home suspension when they might have had to work and been unable to stay home with their child. You might want to ask me at this point, what I did in the winter months when it was freezing outside. I solicited projects from my staff that needed to be completed. The result was a much cleaner building both inside and outside. Bleacher seats were sanded. Built-up wax along the edges of hallways was scraped. There was always something that needed to be done.

That spring, two of our wrestlers cut down two of our trees that were outside of the building. The wrestlers did this because the football players had done the same thing earlier in the year in the back of the building. I could not get anyone to confess to this act of destruction, but I became creative and offered a monetary reward to the first student who told the police who did it. We had students running to the police station to turn in the two miscreants. We now had the names of the two kids who did this. They were both seniors and they were in serious trouble. Their punishment was Saturday school for the rest of the year, replacement of the two trees they cut down, and they had to pay the reward money that I offered to catch them. Word spread among the troops over this punishment and we never had a recurrence of this type of incident. Yes, I could have easily suspended them for ten days and taken them to an expulsion hearing. But why should I ruin their school record for being stupid? Their parents appreciated our willingness to work with them and they completed their senior year without further disruptions. Having the penalty fit the crime was one of my trademarks.

With all new things come headaches. The teachers' union filed a grievance with the school board stating that I was taking away the suspension supervision position from a teacher. I was doing the supervision on my own time. I was not being paid a supplemental salary as this position did not exist in the master contract. I continued to do this supervision till the end of my first year, but the Saturday school supervision became a paid position under the new school year's contract and my Saturday supervising came to an end.

Home Suspensions: Students in my school district were suspended at home for offenses like smoking, truancy, and inappropriate language. The at-home suspension could run from one to ten days. Ten days is the maximum punishment that could be given. Personally, I do not like at-home suspensions. The student may be unsupervised and/or they are just killing time. I would rather have them do an in-school or Saturday school suspension where I could talk with them one-on-one and hopefully find out if there is an underlying cause to their misbehavior. Punishment is more effective if it helps you correct the cause of the behavior, so you do not have a reoccurrence.

Expulsions: Expulsion from school is usually for a semester or if the offense occurs in the second semester for the rest of the school year and can sometimes carry over into the next school year. You will need to build a cumulative discipline report of what the student did wrong, and how they were punished. This should be a rather extensive report as expulsion is a very serious punishment. Generally, you would recommend expulsion for such things as truancy, major theft, and assault of another student. **Neither you nor your assistant can expel a student. Only the superintendent has this authority and the school board must approve it.**

If an expelled student comes onto the campus grounds, they can be charged by the police with criminal trespass. I hope at this point you are seeing the seriousness of an expulsion. This is serious stuff. You need to build a solid case against the student to get this accomplished.

There are other options available to you. The student may see the light and realize they are going to be expelled, so they might simply withdraw from school if they are already eighteen years old. In other cases, where the student is not yet eighteen, the parent simply withdraws them from the school and enrolls them in a private or charter school. In any event, once they are expelled or removed, your problem is solved for the moment. An expulsion, however, does not last forever. This same student can re-enroll at the beginning of the next school year.

EXCEPTIONS: Today, if a child brings a weapon onto your campus, they will be AUTOMATICALLY expelled. No questions asked. Read and memorize the board of education policies on this.

This logically brings us to the question of school security. I had school resource officers on my campus daily. They would start in the parking lots and their mere presence kept the school atmosphere quite subdued. They would then report to the cafeteria area for all the lunch periods and finally return to the parking lots at the end of the day. This is an area that may change drastically as weapons and shootings at school have become more prevalent. Ask any of your assistant principals who they think are most likely to bring a weapon to school. They should be able to give you names immediately. Those are the kids whose lockers should get checked by the assistant principals regularly. When opening a student locker, bring one of your officers as a witness. If you get lucky and find something, confiscate it and put it away in your office. At this point notify the superintendent. Then, have the resource officer accompany you as you go to the student's classroom and take them to your office. Once in the office, confront the student, tell them what they are being charged with, and have them arrested and taken to the police station. Next, notify the parents and explain what has happened. There will be a school board policy in place for you to follow.

Another security measure I would enforce would be to limit the number of doors you can use to enter the building. Once school had started and all the kids were in class, we would close the doors and they were locked to the outside, but for safety reasons, students could always open them from the inside. If a parent or a stranger came to the front door, they would be greeted by the hall aid on duty, given a visitor's badge, and signed in. Our job is to set and enforce policies and procedures to keep everyone safe and prevent school violence.

You will develop a relationship with several students who will rat-out other kids. As these snitches hear these rumors, they can let you know via text or email what they have heard. Sometimes, the student who has a grudge and wants to act out will post their intentions on social media.

Teachers and students who are on the social media sites will be able to give you a heads-up; you will never have a dull day.

<u>THE PISSER AND THE PISSEE</u>: I am now going to recount the story of what we came to entitle, "The Pisser and the Pissee." I had two students who were in swim class and at the end of the lesson went to change in the pool locker room. Our pool was heavily chlorinated, and the kids would shower after class. On this day, one of the boys urinated on another student. Thus, the epic title, "The Pisser and the Pissee" hereafter referred to as the perpetrator and the victim. This was one for the history books, but it really happened. The victim demanded the perpetrator be arrested for assault and be checked for AIDS. Well, now it gets complicated. We suspended the perpetrator. We called the victim's parents but noticed something funny. Their address was not within our school boundary set up by the school district. We called them to come in and they met with me. This event occurred when I had all-female assistants and I thought it might be better for me, as a male, to handle this situation. Well, the parents came in and they were hot. They were screaming and yelling and using the "F" word repeatedly, making a scene as soon as they entered the building. I had to get the police to calm them down and come into my office. Now it gets interesting. These people were not the victim's parents. His parents were deceased, and this was his brother's wife who stepped-up and took the victim and his sister into their home. They were not legal guardians, nor had they petitioned the court to become the legal guardians. With all of that said, we withdrew the victim from our school and recommended to the parents that they obtain legal counsel and guardianship. The brother, his wife, and the victim left my office very unhappy, but we did what was necessary under the law.

YOU NEVER KNOW WHAT YOU ARE GOING TO UNCOVER IF YOU DO A THOROUGH INVESTIGATION.

The other big problem we encountered was fights. After about the first ten days of school in the fall, when kids were starting to settle in and get the lay of the land, we would experience an outbreak of fights. These fights were caused by what went on in the summer and the kids brought their spats into the school. The culminating event was that on Halloween, the kids wore costumes to school. Do not, I repeat *do not* allow high school kids to wear costumes to school, or at least do not allow them to wear masks. Two of our finest students came dressed up as characters from the movie *Dead Presidents*. They consumed a bottle of Jack Daniels and they got into a fight in the cafeteria. Our school resource officer jumped in to break up the fight and, as a result, was punched by one of the students. So, unfortunately, what started as a fun day of wearing costumes at school ended in a student being arrested for assault of an officer. After this, the administration and I decided to enact a new rule that anyone involved in (not just initiating) fighting would immediately receive a ten-day suspension. We also put up cameras at each end of the cafeteria and put our head boys' basketball coach and our head football coach in charge of the two biggest lunch periods. This helped to bring the fighting problem under control. The student who was arrested by the police turned his life around and was later inducted into our school's Hall of Fame. The Hall of Fame induction was reserved for any graduate who did something outstanding with their life after graduation. Who would have imagined that outcome?

My final word on discipline: you will develop a relationship with your students. I say *your* students because you and the assistant principals will have the kids for discipline all four years. You will be able to get to know their families, their problems, and their successes. Graduation can be a very dramatic time for you and the assistant principals because you can see the growth of each of the graduates from their first day as freshmen to their final day when they receive their diploma.

WHEN YOU BEGIN YOUR PRINCIPALSHIP, THE SCHOOL WILL HAVE A DISCIPLINE CODE IN PLACE. YOU NEED TO READ THIS OVER VERY CAREFULLY AND MAKE CHANGES VERY CAUTIOUSLY.

GREAT GUIDELINE #12
SCHOOLS IN THE 2020s

MAIN POINT:

THIS IS GOING TO BE THE MOST CONTROVERSIAL SECTION THAT I HAVE EVER WRITTEN. I AM GOING TO BULLET POINT ALL THE CHANGES THAT I BELIEVE ARE NECESSARY TO IMPROVE THE AMERICAN PUBLIC EDUCATIONAL SYSTEM. THESE BULLET POINTS ARE GOING TO BE THE BASIS OF MY NEXT BOOK WHERE I WILL EXPLAIN IN DETAIL HOW TO EXECUTE THEM.

★ Under the Department of Education and State Superintendents, develop a national committee to select learning standards at every grade level.

★ States will still be responsible for educational financing but only up to a certain level.

★ The federal government will provide additional money for teachers' salaries. There will be a national pay scale with yearly increases and vacations set into the model.

★ Eliminate all teacher unions as there will be nothing left to negotiate.

★ All teachers will become year-round employees.

★ Physical safety will be a top priority.

★ Police will secure all school buildings.

★ Nurses will be on hand to handle all medical problems.

★ Building schedules will be adapted to specific communities and the school year schedule will be flexible.

★ Develop a student-development plan for each student, not just the students in the special education program; not an IEP, but specific goals and measures for the student to work on during the nine weeks of school based on their standardized testing. I have a copy of the Student Development Form at the end of this book. A special thank you to Mr. Richard Lukich, President of Constellation Schools for allowing me to use this document.[5]

★ Utilize school buildings for adult education in the evenings.

★ Develop more English as a Second Language programs.

★ All high schools will teach Spanish, French, German, Mandarin Chinese, and Arabic.

★ Elementary and middle schools will be encouraged to teach these languages; taking a language class will be a graduation requirement for all high schools.

★ School swimming pools and tracks will be open to the public for free.

★ Welcome the community. Do not turn them away.

★ Eliminate school levies for funding and back the school committee fundraising.

★ Develop a strong local PTA and PTA Council.

★ Have a uniform dress code for all students and teachers.

★ Restore and expand vocational education opportunities.

★ Encourage and demand that students attend the local community college and earn free college credit.

---

5   Richard Lukich, "Student Development Plan" (Parma, Ohio: Constellation Schools, 2005).

★ Reinforce through signage throughout the school building—inside and out—that the administration is proud of our staff and students.

★ Redo all bathroom facilities in the building to a single occupancy bathroom open to all students no matter how they identify sexually.

★ There should be a smoke detector in all bathrooms.

★ All bathrooms will be required to be handicap accessible.

★ Make school challenging, fun, and the center of the community.

★ Expand school choice and charter schools; give parents options.

With that all said, I am sure that I will not be looked upon kindly by the teachers' unions. One of the main objectives of teacher unions is reducing teacher contract hours or the amount of work expected within the agreed-upon hours. Teachers need to be highly educated so we will have to develop a plan for teachers to have some time in the summer (as opposed to the school year) to attend graduate school. But a master's degree is no longer enough. They must become experts in their subjects to deliver the best instruction possible. Besides holding a graduate degree, teachers should continually take courses keeping them up to date in their field both for their subject matter and for education itself (pedagogy, classroom management, etc.). Teachers currently are required to take classes to renew or upgrade their state teaching certificates. Perhaps, we should examine what kind of courses they are taking, and which ones are truly beneficial.

The biggest question is where will the money come from? Do you realize that most of the major school districts in this country are underserving their students? Local school districts across the nation are spending record amounts of money on a per-pupil basis and yet the test scores continue to drop. Yet no one comes forward with solutions. Why not? Will it take too long? Is it impossible to fix? Do we not have the time or ability to do improve our test scores? If we do not initiate action, we will continue with mediocrity in our school system and cheat our most precious assets—our children.

Are our children not entitled to a better education? We have spent trillions of dollars in wars overseas that we have no business fighting. The money spent on these wars certainly could have financed what I am suggesting in the bulleted list. Just recently the United States spent over a trillion dollars on the COVID-19 Stimulus Package. Where did this money come from? We simply printed more money.

As a country, we must be the leaders in education. We must prepare our students for the coming decades. If we continue to do the same tired thing year after year and expect different results, we are fools. The public school where I worked was resistant to change. For example, I was named head of the uniform committee in 1995. I gathered up all the information, did my research and due diligence, and was ready to go. I called the superintendent and asked when I should organize and call a meeting of this committee. She told me to call the meeting when I was given specific instructions from her. The call never came. To this day, there are no uniforms in this district.

After I retired from teaching public school, I took a position teaching at Baldwin-Wallace College; it was a wonderful experience. My good friend Dr. Patrick Cosiano brought me on board to supervise student teachers and ultimately, I oversaw student teacher placements. This led to a two-year non-tenured position teaching year-round for the university. I enjoyed it greatly as I felt that I was giving young college students the benefit of my experiences. Unfortunately, I found the college did not allow the student teachers to discuss any other ideas about teaching except those being taught by the college. When Dr. Cosiano retired they appointed a new dean and I was on the move.

I became the principal of a charter elementary school that seemed to embody many of the values and rules that I believed necessary to running a first-rate school. They had a mission statement. They had a dress code. They were open to listening to new ideas. I would like to thank Mr. Richard Lukich and Mr. Gerald Preserean for their faith in hiring me as an elementary principal. The experience gave me a new, refreshing, and new perspective on children and education. I was loved and adored by the children in the school because I was visible, and I spoke with the student body daily. I called each student by name, talking, and walking with them in the halls, listening intently. I volunteered to work the school drop-off and pick-up area. Instead of just standing in front of the school, I made a habit of opening the car doors like a valet. In doing so, I helped form relationships with the parents in addition to the children. For those children who took a car to and from school, I was the face of the school as I was the first person to greet them and the last to say good-bye. We had game nights. Seasonal festivals. All kinds of opportunities for children. It was fun again watching these children soak up knowledge like a sponge. In short, this little charter school was the center of the universe for these children. This is what I want to happen in public school education. Children and parents should have the choice of where to send their kids to school. As it stands today, the charter schools are public schools. The regular public schools dislike the charter schools for two reasons: there are no unions to represent the teachers and no dues are being paid to the union. Teachers at the charter schools are given an at-will contract. Simply put, they can be released at any time.

The following are the models by school level that I would create with changes necessary to improve the American public educational system:

ELEMENTARY SCHOOL MODEL
The elementary school model will consist of:
- ★ **Forty children in each grade level. The student to teacher ratio will be 10:1 with ten children per class, and an intervention specialist at each**

grade level. There will be one school psychologist that will split time between one elementary school and one middle school.

★ The building will be a K-3 building with a separate daycare and after school care units.

★ There will be a single-use bathroom in each room.

★ Children will enter and exit through the same door where they will be greeted by a school resource officer. A nurse will be taking temperatures (and children with a fever will be sent home).

★ All students will be in school uniforms. At each school, there will be a uniform exchange run by the PTA where students can exchange sizes if they choose not to purchase a new uniform.

★ All teachers will be full time, year-round employees with health benefits and retirement benefits.

★ The starting salary will be $100,000 with built-in steps over ten years. Also, teachers will receive tuition money for earning advanced degrees and those already having advanced degrees will earn a higher salary.

★ Computer and technological training will begin in kindergarten.

★ The emphasis at all four grade levels will be reading and math.

★ Other subjects such as American and World History and foreign languages will be part of the curriculum. Health will also be a part of the curriculum and will include nutrition and age-appropriate sex education instruction.

★ All children will be taught social etiquette and receive character education throughout the year to not only include kindness but work ethic. "Please" and "thank you" will be the norms.

★ There will be physical education daily (in addition to recess) and music and art at least several times per week. Instrumental music will be introduced in grade three.

★ All children will be pre- and post-tested to advance to the next grade level.

★ Our goal will be that 100 percent of the children will pass the state-run proficiency tests at the end of grade three. Those that do not will begin individualized remediation.

★ All children will have a student development plan which they are working on constantly from day one of the school year.

★ The school year schedule will be developed by the principal and the staff before the start of the school year.

★ The set-up of the school year will be five nine-week instructional modules with time off for holidays including Thanksgiving, Christmas, and Easter and two weeks in the summer.

★ There will be evening activities and events each five-week period for the entire family.

★ Children will take field trips to the professional theater, major orchestra events, and the zoo regularly.

★ Children will take swimming lessons at the local YMCA to learn how to avoid drowning and if possible, learn to go roller skating and ice skating.

★ Teachers will be evaluated annually.

MIDDLE SCHOOL MODEL

The middle school model will consist of:

★ The school will be a fourth and fifth grade set-up.

★ The middle school model will greatly resemble the elementary set-up.

★ There will be forty children in each grade level. The student to teacher ratio will be 10:1 with ten children per class and an intervention specialist at each grade level. There will be one school psychologist that will split time between one elementary school and one middle school.

★ Computer and technological training continue.

★ Emphasis will continue in reading and math.

★ Other subjects such as American and World History, foreign languages will continue to be part of the curriculum. Health will also be part of the curriculum and will include nutrition and age-appropriate sex education instruction.

★ Every child will have a student development plan to address specific educational issues.

★ Art and music several times per week.

★ Introduction of sports and athletics through intramurals.

★ Teachers will be evaluated annually.

JUNIOR HIGH SCHOOL MODEL

The junior high school model will consist of:

★ The junior high would be a separate building for grades sixth, seventh, and eighth. There will be a total of four classes at each grade level consisting of fifteen students per class, for a 15:1 student to teacher ratio, for a total of sixty children per grade level. There will be two intervention specialists and two psychologists per building.

★ Children will enter and exit through the same door where they will be greeted by a school resource officer and a nurse will be taking temperatures (children with a fever will be sent home).

★ The school year schedule will mirror the other schools' schedules.

★ There will be a full-time art, vocal music, and instrumental music programs.

★ Students will begin to switch classes.

★ There will be physical education multiple times per week.

★ There will be a required life skills class covering topics such, as checkbooks, banking, budgeting, ironing, laundry, and all other basic life skills.

★ Introduction of competitive sports.

HIGH SCHOOL MODEL

The high school model will consist of:

★ The high school would be a separate building for grades ninth, tenth, eleventh, and twelfth.

★ The high school model will consist of five classes for each grade level consisting of twenty students per class, for a 20:1 student to teacher ratio, with a total of 100 students per grade level. If you have more students than this, then you start a second-high school. There will be to intervention specialists and two school psychologists per building.

★ It will be a traditionally run high school with class offerings in English, math, world and American history, foreign language, physical education, band, choir, and health which would include sex education.

★ Children will be taught hygiene. They will shower after gym class and be taught to use deodorant.

★ Children will have post-secondary options at local junior colleges and the opportunity to attend vocational schools.

★ **Students will be prepped for the ACT and SAT and will have opportunities for college visitations.**

★ **All traditional social events will continue such as school dances to include homecoming and prom (and after prom).**

★ There will be a local board of education that oversees the entire operation. The Board will approve purchases and expenses throughout the year but will not have the authority to make extra or new rules for the district. This will come from the Federal Model for Schools.

As you can see, this will be a very expensive educational system to run. However, if we can afford, as a country, to finance wars abroad for trillions of dollars and to give trillions of dollars in stimulus packages, how can we not afford to do this for our most precious commodity? If we continue to do what we have done in the past, will we not get the same results? Where will the money come from? The local district will have a set amount to contribute. The difference will be provided by the Federal government with no strings attached. The National Education Association (NEA) will have a limited role in this program. The local Board of Education will pay a part of the teachers' salary and the federal government will make up the difference to get the teachers to that starting figure of $100,000. We need to elevate the status of teachers and this will help them to achieve that. higher wage. There will be no teacher unions and no dues of any kind to the national, state, or local organizations. Money from the federal government will go directly to the local school districts for the construction of the school buildings. By making teachers year-round we eliminate the argument that they only work 184 days, not a full year.

WE WILL ELEVATE TEACHERS BACK TO A NATIONALLY PRESTIGIOUS POSITION—ONE WHERE TEACHERS ARE HONORED, REVERED, AND RESPECTED.

This will have implications for colleges and how they prepare their student teachers. We need to have super, expert teachers who can and will deliver the goods to students. Therefore, colleges need to rethink their instructional presentation with more of an emphasis on teacher style, teacher presentation, and technology, and computer training.

College professors need to do their job and train these college students to become expert teachers. The professors should be required to use appropriate texts and give appropriate lectures. They should not have tenure nor should they hold a position for life; they should be evaluated annually. College tuition costs should be cut to zero. They should only charge for room and board. I would love to see a return to where the college student had a professor to act as their mentor and guided them through their four years of undergraduate work. I would like to acknowledge Dr. Ruby Redinger who was my mentor, friend, and faculty advisor at Baldwin-Wallace College. She listened and offered appropriate options to me which changed my career. She had me enroll in a theater class in my junior year which led to me writing plays and musicals, culminating in my being part of the original Greenbrier Theatre which is known today as the Cassidy Theatre. I was able to be an assistant principal by day and a musician and play director by night.

CONSTELLATION COMMUNITY SCHOOLS

STUDENT DEVELOPMENT PLAN

Student's Name _____

Teacher's Name _____

Area of Concern _____

Goal #1 _____

_____

_____

Plan of Action: _____

_____

_____

_____

Follow Up: _____

_____

_____

Date of Conference _____

Teacher's Signature _____

Parent's Signature _____

Board Approved 8/19/05

"Constellation Community Schools – The Right Choice for Parents and a Real Chance for Children."

CONSTELLATION COMMUNITY SCHOOLS

STUDENT DEVELOPMENT PLAN

To ensure that all students are successful, we will develop identifiable goals and establish a Student Development Plan for every student. This plan will be based on a Child's prior year's schoolwork, their Stanford test scores and previous teacher's input. By the first Parent conference, each teacher will have developed at least one goal for each of their students. This goal will identify the area for improvement and will have concrete, measurable goals. The goal(s) will be shared with each child's parent/guardian, who will be asked to assist in its implementation.

Board Approved 7/21/05

ABOUT THE AUTHOR

J **ohn D. Roberts** was born in Philadelphia and went to college in Ohio where he stayed for forty-one years working in public education as an athletic director, an assistant and deputy principal, and a principal. He then went to teach at Baldwin-Wallace University for three years and finished his career at a charter school district as an elementary principal and curriculum coordinator. While there, John created the curriculum guide for the charter school district's high school. He has been awarded a PTA State Lifetime Award and a National PTA Lifetime Award. John retired in December of 2019 and moved to Lady Lake, Florida, where he currently resides.

BIBLIOGRAPHY

Gewirtz, David. "Technology That Changed Us: The 1970s, from Pong to Apollo." ZDNet, June 28, 2019. https://www.zdnet.com/.

Lukich, Richard. "Student Development Plan." Parma, Ohio: Constellation Schools, 2005.

Villegas, Tim. "A Brief History of Special Education." Web log. *Think Inclusive* (blog), June 29, 2017. https://www.thinkinclusive.us/brief-history-special-education/.

Wong, Harry K., and Rosemary Wong. *The First Days of School: How to Be an Effective Teacher*. Mountainview, CA: Harry K. Wong Publications, Inc., 2009.

Printed in the USA
CPSIA information can be obtained
at www.ICGtesting.com
JSHW022343140824
68134JS00019B/1665